원서 술술 읽는
Smart Reading 2

원서 술술 읽는 Smart Reading 2

지은이 넥서스영어교육연구소
펴낸이 안용백
펴낸곳 (주)넥서스

출판신고 1992년 4월 3일 제311-2002-2호 ①
121-893 서울시 마포구 양화로 8길 24
Tel (02)330-5500 Fax (02)330-5555

ISBN 979-11-5752-511-9 54740
      979-11-5752-509-6 (SET)

www.nexusEDU.kr
NEXUS Edu는 (주)넥서스의 초·중·고 학습물 전문 브랜드입니다.

원서 술술 읽는
Smart Reading

넥서스영어교육연구소 지음

2

NEXUS Edu

Introduction

Dear Students,

Language learning is a part of your journey to academic success. It can open up many doors and provide you with many opportunities for your future. All four skills (reading, writing, listening and speaking) are important, but reading may be the skill that is most critical to your success in both general language learning as well as test-taking. You are certainly going to face more tests as you continue in school, and reading is the key to doing well on those tests. Indeed, research has shown that reading has the greatest effect on overall language learning success and is the most important factor in getting high TOEFL scores.

Smart Reading is composed of high-interest passages that explore unusual, fascinating topics to spark your imagination. At the same time it focuses on the language you will need for academic success and the language you will use as your language learning journey continues.

Smart Reading is designed to increase your enjoyment of reading, improve your grammar skills, increase your vocabulary and help you comprehend what you read more effectively and efficiently. For each passage there is a pre-reading activity that will give you some interesting facts about the topic and prepare your mind to process the information in the passage. The questions after each passage and the review exercises at the end of each unit will enable you to begin to master the types of questions you will encounter in tests like the foreign language high school exam, the TOEFL test, and the Korean SAT.

We hope you enjoy the passages in this book and we hope the varied and extensive exercises will help you achieve success in English and in your academic future.

Composition of the Book

Reading Passages:

Each book is composed of 32 passages which give students knowledge of various and useful topics. Vocabulary and English structures in each passage are designed to help students not only improve their reading skills but also foster their logical thinking skills.

Pre-reading Activity:

Pre-reading Activity gives students some interesting facts about the topic and hints on what the passage is about.

Reading Tips:

Reading Tips are designed to give students useful expressions or additional interesting information. Through the Reading Tips, students get the opportunity to study useful idioms, phrasal verbs, and grammar.

Comprehension Questions:

Comprehension Questions of various types are designed to help students prepare for the Korean SAT, TOEFL, and foreign language high school exams. Students can check how well they understand each passage and they can also master the types of questions they will encounter on these exams.

Unit Review:

Students have a chance to review the words and the expressions that they have been exposed to in the passages. They can also practice grammar that is crucial to enhancing reading skills.

Table of Contents

UNIT 1
01
02

INTRIGUING CULTURES

Reindeer in the Sami Culture ⊙ 6

First to the Americas ⊙ 8

Unit Review ⊙ 10

UNIT 2
01
02

GOING DEEP

The Deepest Mine in the World ⊙ 12

An Underground Everest ⊙ 14

Unit Review ⊙ 16

UNIT 3
01
02

ANCIENT STRUCTURES

El Castillo: The Castle Pyramid ⊙ 18

The Hanging Gardens of Babylon ⊙ 20

Unit Review ⊙ 22

UNIT 4
01
02

FASHION UPDATES

Bamboo Clothing ⊙ 24

The Evolution of Clothing ⊙ 26

Unit Review ⊙ 28

UNIT 5
01
02

ORGANIC FARMING

An Overview of Organic Farming ⊙ 30

Economic Viability of Organic Farming ⊙ 32

Unit Review ⊙ 34

UNIT 6
01
02

MIND TRICKS

Absent-Minded Genius ⊙ 36

Tricks of the Mind ⊙ 38

Unit Review ⊙ 40

UNIT 7 **THE WORLD OF ART**

Viral Art ⊙ 42

Art Collage ⊙ 44

Unit Review ⊙ 46

UNIT 8 **PEOPLE AND ANIMALS**

Snakes: A Good Story ⊙ 48

The Sanctuary ⊙ 50

Unit Review ⊙ 52

UNIT 9 **EMERGING JOBS IN THE 21ST CENTURY**

What about Becoming a Zoologist? ⊙ 54

Predicting the Future & Future Jobs ⊙ 56

Unit Review ⊙ 58

UNIT 10 **YOUTH TRADITIONS**

Rites of Passage ⊙ 60

The American Prom ⊙ 62

Unit Review ⊙ 64

UNIT 11 **BUTTERFLIES AND MOTHS**

Butterfly Beauties ⊙ 66

The Deceptive Moth ⊙ 68

Unit Review ⊙ 70

UNIT 12 **SAVING THE EARTH**

The Enhanced Greenhouse Effect ⊙ 72

Environmental Solutions ⊙ 74

Unit Review ⊙ 76

▶▶

Table of Contents

 UNIT 13 01 02

TECHNOLOGY

CIA Gadgets—Past and Present ⊙ 78

The Copenhagen Wheel ⊙ 80

Unit Review ⊙ 82

 UNIT 14 01 02

POLITICAL SCIENCE IN ACTION

The Berlin Wall and Its Legacy ⊙ 84

Tiananmen Square ⊙ 86

Unit Review ⊙ 88

 UNIT 15 01 02

LIVING CREATURES

Does the Earth Breathe? ⊙ 90

What Do Plants Like? ⊙ 92

Unit Review ⊙ 94

 **UNIT 16** 01 02

FAMILY

The Changing Family ⊙ 96

The Changing Face of Marriage ⊙ 98

Unit Review ⊙ 100

정답 및 해설

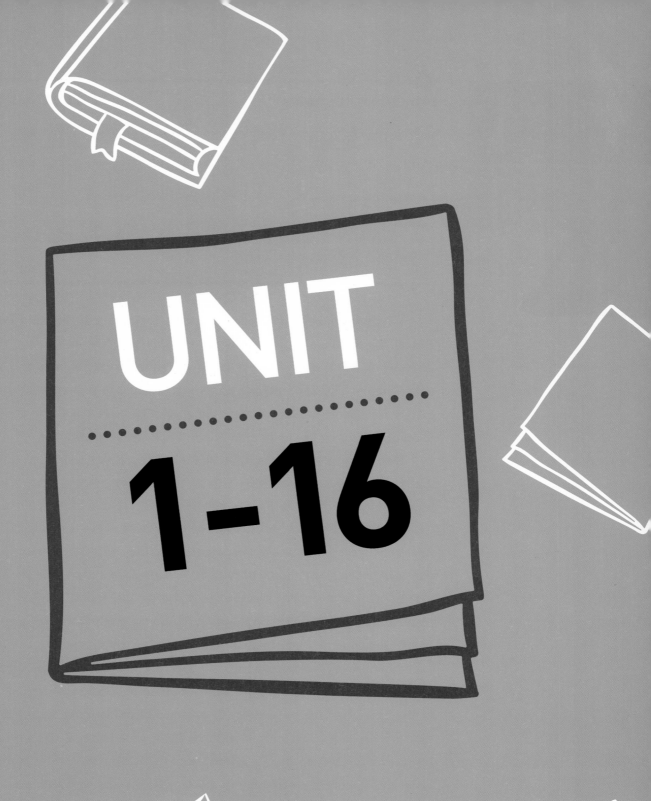

UNIT
1-16

INTRIGUING CULTURES
Reindeer in the Sami Culture

Pre-reading Activity

Livestock are animals kept by people under agricultural conditions for the production of meat, eggs, dairy, or other products. Circle the animals you know are commonly raised as livestock in your country.

| chicken | camel | goat | pig | rabbit |
| sheep | horse | cow | llama | buffalo |

Inhabiting northern Sweden, Norway, Finland, and the Kola Peninsula of Russia, the Sami are one of the largest indigenous groups in Europe. Much of the area they live in is above the Arctic Circle—a harsh environment known for long, cold winters. The Sami people are nomads, and one important feature of their culture is reindeer herding. Some experts have recently stated that the Sami's link to reindeer herding can be traced back as far as 30,000 years.

During the long winters, food and other necessities were <u>scarce</u>. As a result, the Sami found a use for every part of the reindeer. While alive, reindeer were used as a means of transportation and were also a source of milk. Once a reindeer was butchered, every single part was eaten or used in some manner. The reindeer intestines were particularly important since they provided vitamins that were unavailable elsewhere. Some of their body parts were and are still used for sewing together the Sami's cone-shaped tents called Laitok. Today, reindeer meat is very popular among Scandinavians. Sautéed reindeer is one of the most popular dishes. Even reindeer antlers generate income. The antlers are ground to a fine powder and exported to Asian countries, where it is sold as a popular nutritional supplement.

Although the Sami people have adapted to modern society, the reindeer herding industry continues to be important to them. Approximately ten percent of the Sami are connected with reindeer husbandry, including 2,800 who are actively involved full-time. In many regions, only the Sami people who can prove their lineage to a reindeer herding family can legally own and herd reindeer.

Like many traditional industries, reindeer husbandry is under threat from a number of sources, including oil exploration and the wider effects of global warming. _____, the Sami are working hard to maintain <u>this key characteristic</u> of their cultural identity.

Reading Tips

The Sami people are one of the largest indigenous ethnic groups in Europe. They have inhabited the northern regions of Fenno-Scandinavia and Russia for at least 2,500 years. The total population of the Sami is roughly 80,000 to 135,000. More than half of them now are settled in Norway. The Sami have traditionally developed many types of livelihoods such as fur trapping, sheep herding, and coastal fishing. Among them, the best known Sami livelihood is semi-nomadic reindeer herding.

1   **What is the passage mainly about?**

a. the inhabitants of the Nordic countries
b. the nomadic lifestyle of the Sami people
c. the Scandinavians and their use of reindeer
d. the problems faced by the Sami in modern society
e. the close ties between the Sami and the reindeer

2   **Which is closest in meaning to the word "scarce"?**

a. chilly
b. covered
c. insufficient
d. abundant
e. critical

3   **Which best fits in the blank?**

a. Instead
b. In the end
c. Furthermore
d. Nevertheless
e. On top of that

4   **Which of the following is true?**

a. The Sami people live in countries in southern Europe.
b. Reindeer meat is popular and exported to Asian countries.
c. Anyone who is Sami can legally own and herd reindeer.
d. The Sami people are trying to keep their reindeer husbandry.
e. It hasn't been long since the Sami people settled in Europe.

5   **What does the phrase "this key characteristic" refer to?**

_____

INTRIGUING CULTURES

First to the Americas

Pre-reading Activity

True or False?
1. Native Americans migrated from Europe to the Americas.   TRUE   FALSE
2. The first Europeans to reach the Americas were the Vikings B.C. 50.   TRUE   FALSE
3. Starting in the late 16th century, Spain began to colonize eastern North America.   TRUE   FALSE

What can we call the people who came from Asia over 15,000 years ago [1]
and settled throughout the present-day Americas? There are terms such as Native
Americans, First Nations, Indigenous Peoples of the Americas, American Indians,
or simply Indians. In a recent poll among some tribes of Native Americans in the
United States, it was found that *American Indians* came out on top. [5]

While many Americans of European descent try to figure out what the correct
label for the indigenous people is, most of the ancient settlers get a kick out of the
discussion. Quite simply, they do not care what they are called. In fact, there are
thousands of various tribes throughout the Americas—the Navajo Nation in the
southwestern US, the Iroquois of eastern Canada, and the Olmec Nation of Central [10]
America. That is just the tip of the iceberg.

Most scientists today assume these ancient travelers came to the Americas
through Siberia, across the Bering land bridge through Alaska into Canada and
the U.S.A., then down through Central America, and eventually to the tip of South
America. Some of these early wanderers set up camp and stayed in one location, ____ [15]
_____.

Some recent genetic research on DNA of the Incan mummies of Peru found the
Incans are closely related to people from Asia. Another interesting fact is that most
Native Americans have the Mongolian blue birthmark.

The arrival of the Europeans in the late 15th century was not [20]
pleasant for the indigenous tribes. Populations that were
huge across the Americas were decimated due to disease,
warfare, and genocide brought about by the European
colonization. Native American populations declined rapidly
in the first couple of centuries after colonization by the
Spanish, British, French, and others. One disease in
particular—small pox—wiped out 90 percent of the
Native Americans in the state of Massachusetts alone.

Reading Tips

usage of "throughout"

1. in all parts of a particular area, place, etc.
   The disease is prevalent throughout Asia.
   The walls are all painted in pink throughout.

2. during all of a particular period
   She was committed to helping the poor throughout her life.
   He kept nodding off throughout the movie.

1   What is the last paragraph mainly about?

   a. the motives for the European colonization of the Americas
   b. the various tribes that survived the attack of the Europeans
   c. the diseases which were spread among the Native Americans
   d. how the arrival of the Europeans resulted in the mass deaths of Indians
   e. how the first people into the Americas faced the migration of the Europeans

2   What does the underlined phrase "the tip of the iceberg" mean?

   a. an array of hints, tips, and quotes
   b. something which can be easily done
   c. something which conceals its true color
   d. only a hint of something larger or more complex
   e. a problem so controversial and sensitive to deal with

3   Which best fits in the blank?

   a. while others continued heading south
   b. while others started returning to their homelands
   c. while Europeans called them American Indians
   d. while South America was overrun by Europeans
   e. while Europeans continued to come to the Americas

4   Which is closest in meaning to the word "decimated"?

   a. dismissed
   b. massacred
   c. preserved
   d. diagnosed
   e. conquered

5   What can be inferred from the passage?

   a. Some tribes lived in the Americas long before the people from Asia arrived.
   b. The first people into the Americas never made it to the tip of South America.
   c. Ancient travelers used a very big boat when they moved to the American continent.
   d. The American Indians who had lived in South America migrated to the North.
   e. Most Native Americans didn't have antibodies against the diseases brought by Europeans.

A Words

A1. Fill in the blank according to the definition.

peninsula	husbandry	decimate	scarce	descent

1 _____: to kill a lot of people in a particular area

2 _____: insufficient to meet a need or demand; not abundant

3 _____: the production of crops or animals for food or farming

4 _____: a person's hereditary origins; the process of going down

5 _____: an area of land almost completely surrounded by water, but joined at one end to a larger area of land

A2. Choose the most appropriate word for each blank.

1 They have been looking for a suitable _____ for their new house.
   a. location   b. research   c. situation   d. supervision

2 The _____ of Australia by the English occurred over 200 years ago.
   a. competition   b. transportation   c. colonization   d. adaptation

3 There is simply no _____ value in most snack foods on the market today.
   a. educational   b. logical   c. international   d. nutritional

4 Li Feng was able to trace her _____ to Taipei, on the island of Taiwan.
   a. smell   b. footage   c. English   d. lineage

5 Recently, a study revealed a _____ link between humans and Neanderthals.
   a. profitable   b. genetic   c. lucid   d. necessary

A3. Complete each sentence with one of the words from the box.

antlers	genocides	terms	harsh	nomads

1 Many people think the _____ from deer have great health benefits.

2 Some scientific _____ are hard to pronounce even for a professional.

3 As _____, they travel from the plains of Mongolia to upper Mongolia.

4 The organization is dedicated to helping children living in _____ conditions.

5 The African continent has experienced far too many _____ in the past few centuries.

B

Expressions and Phrases

B1. Fill in the blank using an expression from the box.

as a result	under threat	a number of	due to

1 Our oceans are continually _____ as temperatures and acid levels rise.
2 The financial crisis is still ongoing, and _____, home sales are still low.
3 They decided to lay off half of their workers _____ financial difficulties.
4 There have been _____ outbreaks in the area, so they don't have clean water.

B2. Complete each sentence with an expression from the reading passages.
   (Change the form of the verb if necessary.)

bring about	figure out	be related to	wipe out

1 Can you help me _____ what's wrong with my computer?
2 The genetic record shows that Homo sapiens _____ chimpanzees.
3 Many people believe we can _____ global poverty within 150 years.
4 The social change _____ by the Industrial Revolution was significant.

C

Summary

Complete the summary with the appropriate words and expressions.

arrival	harsh	tribes	settled
important	nomads	herding	ancient

The Sami people of northern Europe live in a(n) _____ environment, and they are famous for reindeer _____. There is evidence that these _____ have been working with reindeer for over 30,000 years. The reindeer play a(n) _____ part in Sami culture and history.

Over 15,000 years ago, _____ travelers from Asia came over the Bering land bridge into the Americas and _____ throughout the new continents. Thousands of _____ spread throughout the continents and settled here and there. The _____ of the Europeans in the late 15th century was not pleasant for the indigenous settlers.

GOING DEEP
The Deepest Mine in the World

Pre-reading Activity

Fill in the blanks using the following words: *environment*, *potential*, and *valuable*

Mining is the industry of getting _____ minerals or other geological materials from the earth. But the nature of mining processes creates some _____ negative effects on the _____ both during the mining operations and for years after the mine is closed.

Seventy kilometers from Johannesburg, South Africa, a company named Gold Fields Ltd. is drilling a mine that will go down over four kilometers. When completed, it will be the world's deepest mine. ___(A)___, the TauTona mine, also in South Africa, almost reached 3.9 kilometers in depth by 2008, and this made it the deepest mine in the world. This extreme mining is literally part of a new gold rush, with companies risking the dangers of ever deeper mines in pursuit of valuable metals whose prices keep rising.

Gold, a precious metal used in everything from jewelry to the electrical systems of airplanes and spacecrafts, now trades at well over 1,000 U.S. dollars per ounce. With gold prices this high, companies are now mining deposits of the metal that were once too deep and expensive to extract. The newest and deepest areas of the TauTona mine, ___(B)___ an estimated 8.5 million ounces of gold are thought to exist, can take up to one hour to reach from the surface. Nearly 5,600 miners work there, laboring to bring the precious gold up from this underworld.

At these depths, gold mining becomes very dangerous. At the bottom of the mines this far down in the earth, the air temperature can reach 60 degrees Celsius. One can imagine the size and power of air conditioners needed to allow miners to work safely. Ventilation is also very important to clear out toxic fumes from the explosions and heavy machinery used in the mining operation. Despite these precautions, deep mines remain a hazardous place to work. Every year, there are deaths at TauTona and other mines that operate this far down.

Operating the deepest mine in the world is a risky and expensive business, but with shallower deposits of gold already mined and the price of gold ever rising, it seems the only way to go is down.

Reading Tips

the basic units for measuring weight

grain: 0.06 grams (the smallest unit for measuring weight, used for weighing medicines)

ounce: 28.35 grams

pound: 454 grams

ton: 907,200 grams

1 **What is the third paragraph mainly about?**

a. the necessity for mine development

b. a variety of precautions against accidents

c. a very risky working environment for miners

d. the tragic deaths that occur in these deep mines

e. the importance of safety facilities in South Africa

2 **Which is closest in meaning to the word "extract"?**

a. separate

b. destroy

c. contain

d. estimate

e. suppress

3 **Which best fits in the blanks?**

	(A)		(B)
a.	However	⋯	whom
b.	Therefore	⋯	where
c.	As a result	⋯	which
d.	For example	⋯	that
e.	Meanwhile	⋯	where

4 **Which of the following is NOT true?**

a. Companies take some risk in order to look for gold.

b. Gold is used in a diverse range of industrial applications.

c. With gold prices going up, miners are going down deeper to find gold.

d. The temperature of the deepest area of the TauTona mine is very high.

e. The deep mines are not a hazardous place to work any more thanks to the safety precautions.

5 **Why do we need to purify the air in underground mines?**

_____

An Underground Everest

Pre-reading Activity

Look at the title of the passage, and circle the words you think will be in the passage.

horizontal   spelunkers   open-ended   equipment   deepest   blockage
expand   squeeze   mountain   exploration   ceiling   geologist

Now scan the passage, and see if you were right. How many? _____

The Voronya Cave, in the Caucasus Mountains in the country of Georgia, is the world's deepest cave. It is greater than 2,000 meters deep, and reaching the bottom has proven difficult. It was not even entered until the early 1960s, when a Georgian cave explorer—a spelunker—made a brief exploration to about 60 meters. (1)

In 1982, a group of Ukrainian spelunkers from Kiev began digging through cave blockages in order to explore the Voronya Cave more deeply. They eventually descended to 340 meters by 1987. (2) But exploring the cave further proved difficult. There were dead ends that led nowhere, icy waterfalls, and floods pouring freezing water into underground rivers. In addition, there were narrow "squeezes" too small to pass through and vertical drops and shafts of hundreds of meters leading down into darkness where the explorers could not see. On top of that, political and ethnic conflict in the region began in 1992 and did not stabilize until 1998. This caused the exploration of the cave to be delayed. (3)

Finally, in the 2000s, a series of expeditions named "the Call of the Abyss" began <u>systematically</u> exploring the cave, blasting through the narrow squeezes and hauling tons of gear and equipment down on ropes from the surface. (4) A 56-member team spent four weeks reaching a depth of 1,840 meters, followed by a nine-person team that reached a chamber they named "Game Over" more than 2,000 meters down in October, 2004. (5)

The spelunkers compared <u>it</u> to an underground Mt. Everest. No one is yet finished exploring the Voronya. The expedition leader said, "When you explore a cave, you don't know where the final limit lies. Even now, we don't know whether we've reached the limit—or if it will go on. But we are pretty sure we'll eventually go even lower."

Reading Tips

usage of "whether"

1. used when talking about a choice or doubt between alternatives
   I'm not sure whether this is right.

2. used to say that something definitely will or will not happen in any of the circumstances
   I'm in love with him whether you like it or not.

1 What is the passage mainly about?

   a. the findings inside the Voronya Cave
   b. the continued expeditions of the Voronya Cave
   c. social and political conflict in the country of Georgia
   d. the comparison of the Voronya Cave to Mount Everest
   e. the reasons why spelunkers stopped exploring the Voronya Cave

2 Which is closest in meaning to the word "systematically"?

   a. irregularly
   b. methodically
   c. inconsistently
   d. unpredictably
   e. sensitively

3 Where does the following sentence best fit in the passage?

This was the first-ever time a cave of more than two kilometers deep had been explored.

   a. (1)   b. (2)   c. (3)   d. (4)   e. (5)

4 Which best fits in the blanks?

It is hard to _____ how deep the Voronya Cave called an underground Mt. Everest is. But spelunkers have constantly tried to _____ into the underground world in spite of a lot of adversity.

   a. examine, visit   b. imagine, translate   c. locate, live
   d. estimate, venture   e. distinguish, enter

5 What does the word "it" refer to?

   _____

A **Words**

A1. Fill in the blank according to the definition.

| extract | ventilation | vertical | chamber | trade |

1 _____: to draw out or to pull out with force
2 _____: being in a position at right angles to the horizon
3 _____: a compartment or enclosed space under the ground
4 _____: the movement of fresh air around a room or building
5 _____: to exchange something; to buy and sell goods or services

A2. Choose the most appropriate word for each blank.

1 It is very foolish of Jack to waste his _____ time on it!
   a. dangerous   b. access   c. local   d. precious

2 Measures to _____ consumer prices are urgently needed.
   a. stabilize   b. complete   c. weaken   d. eliminate

3 Spraying pesticides and herbicides is _____ for many workers.
   a. confident   b. hazardous   c. predictable   d. shallow

4 The factory has to take every _____ to avoid injuries to workers.
   a. explosion   b. risk   c. precaution   d. carelessness

5 It is impossible to _____ how many people were affected by the civil war.
   a. squeeze   b. estimate   c. compress   d. explode

A3. Complete each sentence with one of the words from the box.

| bottom | spacecraft | expeditions | gear | blockage |

1 The dog ate a tennis ball and had intestinal _____ for days.
2 The campers kept all of their _____ in backpacks out of the rain.
3 Can you hold the _____ of the ladder while I change the light bulb?
4 The travel agency is growing rapidly because of their African _____.
5 Future _____ will orbit the earth's atmosphere more cheaply than today.

B Expressions and Phrases

B1. Fill in the blank using an expression from the box.

up to	in pursuit of	in order to	on top of that

1 I went on a seven-day fast _____ lose five kilograms.
2 Scientists and researchers are _____ a cure for cancer.
3 John scored 24 points, and _____ he had 17 rebounds!
4 Brian continued to care for his grandmother _____ the day she died.

B2. Complete each sentence with an expression from the reading passages.
(Change the form of the verb if necessary.)

bring up	clear out	pass through	go on

1 We had to _____ Kuala Lumpur on our way to Singapore.
2 If we had let the fight _____, one or both of them could have been hurt.
3 There are many treasure seekers who _____ old shipwrecks from the ocean's floor.
4 Before being scolded by your mother, you had better _____ all that junk in your room.

C Summary

Complete the summary with the appropriate words and expressions.

precautions	spelunkers	constantly	deeper
dangerous	underground	reach	proven

There is a gold mine that will _____ down over four kilometers. With gold prices going up, companies are drilling _____ to get the precious metal. Mining gold at these depths is very _____. In spite of safety _____, operating the deepest mine in the world is extremely hazardous work.

The Voronya Cave named a(n) _____ Mt. Everest is the world's deepest cave. Expeditions have _____ made attempts to reach the bottom since the early 1960s, but it has _____ difficult. In 2004, some _____ reached a depth of over 2,000 meters. However, they believed that the cave would go deeper still.

ANCIENT STRUCTURES

El Castillo: The Castle Pyramid

Pre-reading Activity

Did you know?
A pyramid is a large stone structure having triangular outer surfaces that slope in to a point at the top. Although the pyramids in Egypt are best known to us, many ancient civilizations such as Mesopotamia and Mesoamerica (Central America) also built pyramidal structures.

Chichen Itza is a major archeological site located on Mexico's Yucatán Peninsula. Dating back to the 7th century A.D., it is considered one of the most important cities of the ancient Mayan culture. Chichen Itza, now a UNESCO World Heritage Site, is a popular tourist attraction. It contains numerous stone buildings, and many have been beautifully restored. The settlement is dominated by the Temple of Kukulkan, or as it is often called "El Castillo," which is Spanish for "the Castle," at its center.

El Castillo is an excellent example of a step-pyramid. The pyramid is four-sided with steps running up each side to the temple at the top. Each staircase contains 91 steps. If you count the step at the top, they all add up to 365 steps or the number of days in a year. This <u>corresponds</u> to a part of the Mayan calendar called "the Haab." The pyramid is 30 meters high including the six-meter-high temple at the top. On the north staircase there are spectacular sculptures of feathered serpents running down the sides. The name of the Temple, Kukulkan, actually means feathered serpent and was an important god in Mayan mythology.

Tourists may experience the amazing shadows cast by the sculptures, if they pay a visit during the spring or autumn equinox. The entire structure is made up of nine levels. Archeologists believe that this may be linked to the Mayan cosmological belief that there are nine levels in the Mayan "Underworld." The staircase in the center of the pyramid has 13 levels. Experts are of the opinion that this _____ the number of levels in the "Upperworld."

Owing to its extraordinary architectural beauty, El Castillo is the second-most visited archeological site in Mexico. In 2007, it was selected as one of the "New Seven Wonders of the World" after a worldwide vote.

Reading Tips

Equinoxes are the two times during a year when the Sun crosses the plane of the earth's equator. The moment at which the Sun's path crosses the celestial equator moving from south to north is called the vernal equinox. And the autumn equinox is the other way around. Equinoxes make night and day of approximately equal length all over the earth and occur around March 21 and September 23.

1 **What is the second paragraph mainly about?**

   a. diverse examples of step-pyramids

   b. the figure and structure of El Castillo

   c. the snake deity in Mayan mythology

   d. the Haab—the Mayan calendric system

   e. historical considerations of El Castillo

2 **Which is closest in meaning to the word "corresponds"?**

   a. includes

   b. modifies

   c. exchanges

   d. correlates

   e. adheres

3 **Which best fits in the blank?**

   a. combines

   b. represents

   c. stimulates

   d. furnishes

   e. tangles

4 **Which of the following is NOT true about El Castillo?**

   a. It is surrounded by no other ancient sculptures.

   b. It is made up of nine levels and four stairways.

   c. It is a very popular archeological site in Mexico.

   d. It is one of the New Seven Wonders of the World.

   e. It is possibly linked to the Mayan cosmological beliefs.

5 **What can we witness if we visit the Temple of Kukulkan during the equinoxes?**

   _____

The Hanging Gardens of Babylon

Pre-reading Activity

True or false?
1. Babylon was a city-state of the ancient empire of the Incas.	TRUE	FALSE
2. Babylon was located in modern-day Iraq.	TRUE	FALSE
3. The Babylonian civilization reached its ultimate glory in the 7th century B.C.	TRUE	FALSE

The Hanging Gardens of Babylon were located in what is modern-day Iraq. They were one of the original Seven Wonders of the Ancient World and were built by a Babylonian king around 600 B.C. The story goes that the king married a woman from another land called Persia. Unfortunately, the new queen suffered terribly from homesickness. Though she had all the riches any woman could want, she longed for her native land of Persia.

The land of Babylon was dry and <u>barren</u>—exactly like it is today. The queen missed the smells of trees, the fragrances of colorful flowers, and the yummy aroma of fruit trees and their sweet blossoms. _____, the king got the idea of building the most beautiful fragrant gardens in the world. He thought that if he built such gardens with all the lovely smells of Persia, she would most certainly overcome her homesickness.

The Hanging Gardens that the king built shocked travelers to the area. The structures of the Hanging Gardens were very high. The gardens probably did not really "hang" in the sense of being suspended from cables or ropes. They were built on terraces which were part of the ziggurat and were irrigated by water lifted up from the Euphrates. The king applied special technologies to raise the water high into the gardens. The ancient Greek historians wrote extensively about the garden structures. They wrote that the walls to protect the gardens were ten meters thick. In addition, the gardens were built very high with multiple staircases and pathways to travel through them.

There is some controversy as to whether the Hanging Gardens were an actual creation or a poetic creation due to a lack of documentation. The only remains of the gardens are the numerous stories about them that are in ancient texts. Additionally, there are numerous drawings and diagrams. Were they just a legend written about by poets and sketched by artists?

Reading Tips

usage of "as to"

1. used to indicate what a question or piece of information is about
   I was uncertain as to whether the project should be continued or not.

2. used when you are starting to talk about something new that is connected with what was previously mentioned
   As to our strategy, we will focus on small profits and quick returns.

1 **What is the passage mainly about?**

a. a king's attempt to make his queen homesick
b. a queen's life of misery in the land of Babylon
c. a Babylonian king and his devotion to his queen
d. amazing gardens built in Babylon to attract travelers
e. a beautiful structure that a Babylonian king built for his queen

2 **Which is closest in meaning to the word "barren"?**

a. frigid
b. fertile
c. desolate
d. operative
e. capricious

3 **Which best fits in the blank?**

a. To make his land productive
b. To please the saddened queen
c. To plunder the fruitful land of Persia
d. To find a cure for deadly disease
e. To strengthen the Babylonian Empire

4 **What can be inferred from the passage?**

a. It rarely rains in the land of Babylon.
b. The Hanging Gardens were just a myth or legend.
c. The king would probably invade Persia and take it over.
d. The Hanging Gardens made the queen get more homesick.
e. Many people were mobilized to lift water up from the Euphrates.

5 **Which best fits in the blanks?**

> The Hanging Gardens of Babylon were built by a Babylonian king to
> _____ his homesick queen. Trees and flowers were planted on terraces,
> and the Euphrates was used to _____ the plants in the Hanging Gardens
> of Babylon.

a. please, kill   b. escape, sprinkle   c. surprise, log
d. console, water   e. marry, grow

A Words

A1. Fill in the blank according to the definition.

heritage	mythology	controversy	barren	irrigate

1 _____: something passed down from preceding generations
2 _____: incapable of producing seed, fruit, or any other crops
3 _____: a prolonged argument or dispute involving many people
4 _____: to supply water to land or crops through a system of pipes
5 _____: a set of stories, beliefs, or traditions associated with people

A2. Choose the most appropriate word for each blank.

1 I want the beautiful chandelier that is _____ from the ceiling.
   a. refined   b. ceased   c. replaced   d. suspended

2 Some of the exchange students suffered from _____ while abroad.
   a. suspension   b. homesickness   c. fraud   d. amnesia

3 There is _____ evidence that humans ate cereals over 100,000 years ago.
   a. cosmological   b. architectural   c. genetic   d. archeological

4 There is plenty of _____ that proves he legally immigrated to the U.S.A.
   a. extension   b. conviction   c. documentation   d. improvement

5 The museum houses many abstract paintings from the early 1900s which are beautifully
   _____.
   a. generated   b. restored   c. designated   d. repeated

A3. Complete each sentence with one of the words from the box.

attraction	staircase	dominated	cast	temple

1 The automaker _____ the domestic car market last year.
2 The shadows that were _____ on the wall gave me a fright.
3 The _____ built on the rocky hill is an architectural marvel.
4 Turn right at the corner, and take the _____ to the second floor.
5 Disney World is the number one _____ for tourists visiting Florida.

B Expressions and Phrases

B1. Fill in the blank using an expression from the box.

owing to	as to	in addition	lack of

1 I am not sure _____ whether the construction is completed or not.
2 The right-wing party may win the election _____ the immigration issue.
3 The milk from our farm is especially rich in Calcium. _____, it's fat-free.
4 The number of orangutans in Indonesia has gone down rapidly due to a(n) _____
 land and resources.

B2. Complete each sentence with an expression from the reading passages.
 (Change the form of the verb if necessary.)

date back to	add up to	pay a visit	be made up of

1 The number of islands in the Philippines _____ over 7,000.
2 The old pendant found in the royal tomb _____ the 10th century.
3 When we go to Singapore, we are going to _____ to the night zoo.
4 The human body _____ trillions of cells that work together brilliantly.

C Summary

Complete the summary with the appropriate words and expressions.

sculptures	appear	supposedly	Mayan
homesick	archeological	centerpiece	fragrant

El Castillo is the _____ of a World Heritage Site in Mexico known as Chichen
Itza. An important part of the _____ culture, El Castillo is a step-pyramid that
stands 30 meters high, and it has amazing _____ of feathered serpents. With
its mysterious structure and _____ significance, El Castillo is one of the most
visited historic sites in Mexico.

The Hanging Gardens of Babylon, one of the original Seven Wonders of the Ancient
World, were _____ built around 600 B.C. by a king who wanted to please his
_____ queen. The gardens were put up high on terraces with _____
flowers and plants and gave the illusion that they were "hanging" from above. The delicate
gardens now only _____ in books and stories.

FASHION UPDATES

Bamboo Clothing

Pre-reading Activity

Fill in the blanks using the following words: *hardwood*, *incredibly*, *plant*, and *climate*

Bamboo is the fastest-growing woody _____ on Earth. It's as durable as _____, even though the plant is technically in the grass family. Bamboo grows _____ fast. Under the right soil and _____ conditions, it can grow as much as 3 to 5 centimeters per hour.

The next T-shirts, underwear, socks, jeans, sweatshirts, or blouses you buy might not be made of cotton, polyester, or any other popular fabric. They may be made from bamboo. Bamboo is becoming the new eco-friendly choice in the clothing industry. Many fashion experts are wondering if bamboo fabric will be a fad, or if it will be around for a long time. 5

In my opinion, bamboo is here to stay. Bamboo has a natural silky sheen. It is very "breathable" and feels much lighter than the relatively heavy cotton materials. It is also a material that keeps you drier than cotton and other fabrics. Bamboo is naturally UV protective, so this helps minimize the damage that the sun can do to our skin. Another health benefit is that bamboo has antimicrobial <u>properties</u> that 10 destroy some harmful microorganisms such as bacteria and even viruses.

(1) In a time where the environmental impact of products is considered carefully, the most important aspect of bamboo may be its sustainability. (2) Cotton and other natural fabrics take a lot of resources to grow, cultivate, and harvest. Needless to say, polyester and other man-made fabrics are nightmares 15 for the environment. (3) Bamboo, on the other hand, grows really fast compared to other wooden plants. (4) It is more sustainable than most other fabrics and is completely organic. Bamboo does not require nearly as many chemicals like pesticides and herbicides. (5)

From a comfort standpoint, bamboo T-shirts and other clothing articles stay 20 very soft for as long as you wear them. It is pretty easy to see why most fashion people are excited about this new entry into the fabric and clothing industry.

Reading Tips

Bamboos are the fastest growing woody plants in the world. They are able to grow up to 60 cm or more per day due to a unique rhizome-dependent system. But this astounding growth rate highly relies on local soil and climatic conditions. In East Asia and South East Asia, their stems are used extensively in everyday life as building materials and as a highly versatile raw material.

1 **What is the passage mainly about?**

a. eco-friendly fashion using organic techniques
b. benefits of using bamboo and cotton for clothing
c. a comparison between bamboo and other fabrics
d. bamboo clothing: a new fabric choice in eco-fashion
e. positive effects of bamboo fabric on our environment

2 **Which is closest in meaning to the word "properties"?**

a. contents
b. ingredients
c. characteristics
d. possessions
e. valuables

3 **Where does the following sentence best fit in the passage?**

In these respects, bamboo is better for the environment.

a. (1)   b. (2)   c. (3)   d. (4)   e. (5)

4 **Which of the following is NOT true?**

a. Bamboo fabric is rough and changeable.
b. Bamboo naturally functions as a sunblock.
c. Bamboo has antibacterial qualities killing some bacteria.
d. Bamboo grows fast without fertilizers unlike other wooden plants.
e. Bamboo isn't treated with harsh chemicals, so bamboo clothes are good for our health.

5 **Which best fits in the blanks?**

Bamboo fabric has several excellent _____ that cannot be found in other fabrics. Also, bamboo has many environmental _____ and is in the spotlight as an innovative fabric.

a. choices, disadvantages   b. experts, interests   c. chemicals, benefits
d. properties, advantages   e. articles, obstacles

FASHION UPDATES

The Evolution of Clothing

Pre-reading Activity

Look at the title of the passage, and circle the words you think will be in the passage.

| function | fashionable | exist | export | therapy | medicine |
| athlete | impact | magnetic | exhausted | expel | innovation |

Now scan the passage, and see if you were right. How many? _____

In the past, clothing was just about function and fashion. The function was just to cover our bodies with clothing to keep us warm and comfortable. Then, fashion came around to make us "look good." But these days, the entire clothing industry is going through many innovations. One of these innovations revolves around health. Some new clothing lines are being designed in order to be like "_____." 1

How would this look? First off, the ingredients going into clothes are a bit different. Some people claim that there are two kinds of minerals that improve a person's health. One of these minerals comes from a semi-precious stone called tourmaline. Another is a gray stone called magnetite. Magnetite, as its name suggests, is the most magnetic mineral naturally occurring on the planet. It is also popularly worn as jewelry by people who believe in the controversial magnet therapy. Supposedly, if you wear tourmaline and magnetite, your overall health improves. If you are skeptical about this, turn on the TV and watch some professional athletes. Many of today's famous athletes are wearing these minerals as necklaces because they believe this new apparel improves their physical health. In addition, the athletes say they have much greater concentration while wearing wristbands, necklaces, and other trinkets made of tourmaline and magnetite. 5 10 15 20

It was just a matter of time before some fashion designers came up with the idea to grind these semi-precious stones and put the minerals into the fabric of clothing. Initial results are looking very promising. While the scientific community still debates the true power of wearing these items, customers seem to enjoy them very much. 25

Reading Tips

make, have, let + object + verb
to force someone to do something
Our teacher had us clean the science lab after school.
My mother makes me study English every night.
Let me show you a few examples.

1   What is the best alternative title of the passage?

a. New Sports Apparel
b. The Function of New Fashion
c. New Ingredients in Our Clothes
d. The Latest Eco-friendly Trends Lines
e. The Downfall of the Clothing Industry

2   Which best fits in the blank?

a. therapy for stability of our minds
b. costumes for a Halloween party
c. nostalgia for the good old days
d. fashion for extreme sports
e. medicine for the body

3   Which is closest in meaning to the word "ingredients"?

a. quantities
b. occasions
c. processes
d. components
e. suggestions

4   Why does the author mention the underlined word "controversial"?

a. because there is debate about the effectiveness of the magnet therapy
b. because there are many athletes who wear necklaces made of magnetite
c. because there are a lot of people who think magnetite is good for our health
d. because there is controversy over which is better—tourmaline or magnetite
e. because there are many people who believe the magnet therapy is only a temporary fad

5   According to the passage, who is skeptical of this trend?

_____

A Words

A1. Fill in the blank according to the definition.

| skeptical | microorganism | mineral | fabric | grind |

1 _____: doubting things that other people believe
2 _____: cloth or other material produced by weaving or knitting fibers
3 _____: a substance such as gold or coal that is formed naturally in the earth
4 _____: to reduce something to fine particles, usually by pounding or crushing
5 _____: a living thing such as bacteria that is too small to see with the naked eye

A2. Choose the most appropriate word for each blank.

1 You have to _____ the land to get ready for planting this year's crops.
   a. possess   b. cultivate   c. polish   d. leach

2 Due to a(n) _____ drop in sales, the revenue forecast for the year is unfavorable.
   a. extra   b. skeptical   c. feasible   d. overall

3 I invested some of my savings in my son's business since it seemed _____.
   a. hopeless   b. controversial   c. promising   d. discouraged

4 If the project seems to be going nowhere, you need to consider it from a different _____.
   a. standpoint   b. indication   c. corner   d. concentration

5 Animal-assisted _____ is where dogs are used to visit old people to help them feel better.
   a. medicine   b. property   c. industry   d. therapy

A3. Complete each sentence with one of the words from the box.

| debate | comfort | nightmare | chemicals | silky |

1 All the furniture we supply is designed primarily for _____.
2 That new shampoo is amazing. My hair feels so _____ and fresh.
3 The _____ between the two candidates did not reveal any new information.
4 While people don't like us using _____, they are definitely more convenient.
5 I still have the same _____ I had when I was 10 years old, and it's still scary.

B Expressions and Phrases

B1. Fill in the blank using an expression from the box.

in order to	on the other hand	first off	needless to say

1 _____, we must decide who will do each part. Then we can start.

2 _____, the desperate refugees are hoping for aid from donor organizations.

3 The company's new logo is very bright, but _____ the design is not so good.

4 The George Washington Bridge was built _____ connect New York City and New Jersey.

B2. Complete each sentence with an expression from the reading passages. (Change the form of the verb if necessary.)

come around	go through	come up with	turn on

1 The old lady has _____ a lot of hardship living on her own for so long.

2 Either hand me the remote control or please _____ the stereo yourself.

3 The newcomer has _____ a great idea that can be applied to our new program.

4 He'd better not _____ here anymore, or the dogs are going to bite him again.

C Summary

Complete the summary with the appropriate words and expressions.

industry	innovations	advantages	widely
minerals	environmental	act	require

Bamboo is becoming the new choice of fabric in the clothing _____. But people are wondering if bamboo fabric is just a fad. In fact, bamboo has more _____ than any other fabric. Above all, it feels soft and silky and is more sustainable. From a(n) _____ perspective, bamboo is even better since it is organic and does not _____ as many chemicals as cotton or other fibers.

The clothing industry is going through lots of _____, and health is at the center of these new designs. Some _____ such as tourmaline and magnetite are ground and put in clothing in order to _____ like medicine. While still a bit controversial, the trinkets made of these ingredients are _____ worn.

ORGANIC FARMING

An Overview of Organic Farming

Pre-reading Activity

Look at the title of the passage, and circle the words you think will be in the passage.

| profitability | rotation | cost-effective | producer | environmental |
| pesticides | yield | deliberate | livestock | helpful |

Now scan the passage, and see if you were right. How many? _____

The effort to increase yield and profitability on farmlands has required the use of large amounts of chemicals and pesticides. Scientists work with the genes of grains, fruits, and vegetables in order to grow much larger sized produce. In addition, livestock raised on farms are regularly injected with artificial hormones to create more meat per animal. This, of course, affects the livestock's health, and many notice it affects human consumers' health as well. The use of so many other types of chemicals in the grain and livestock industries also does a lot of harm to the environment. In response to these issues, the organic agriculture movement is flourishing.

Organic agriculture has provided a solution to the harmful use of chemicals. Farmers cannot risk losing their crops to insects, but traces of pesticides, even in minute amounts, are not healthy for consumers. Thus, organic farming uses alternative methods. Instead of using chemical sprays, farmers often use bags to cover plants. Also, natural predators are used to fight insect pests. Farmers release tiny pirate bugs, ladybugs, etc. into their farms. Genetically-modified plants are another way to fight insect pests so that <u>they</u> are no longer attracted to the taste or texture of the plants. However, modifying plants genetically is still controversial to those who advocate a completely natural approach to farming.

Farmers use pesticides from natural sources like pyrethrum and rotenone as well. It is very challenging to raise a successful crop without the threat of insect pests, so many choose to use these more effective, yet still <u>controversial</u> methods.

The most important reason for using natural pesticides is to avoid the environmental damage from toxic pesticides that ruin soil and water quality in regions where there are run-offs. Though completely natural methods are not as cost-effective in a market society, there has been significant improvement in organic farming methods.

5

10

15

20

25

Reading Tips

types of grains

maize
rice
wheat
barley
sorghum
millet
oats
rye
triticale
buckwheat

1 **What is the second paragraph mainly about?**

   a. warning on the use of toxic pesticides

   b. a debate about genetically-modified plants

   c. pesticides from nature used in organic farming

   d. natural predators used as substitutes for chemicals

   e. safer alternatives to the harmful chemicals in agriculture

2 **What does the word "they" refer to?**

   a. chemicals

   b. alternative methods

   c. genetically-modified plants

   d. natural predators

   e. insect pests

3 **Which is closest in meaning to the word "controversial"?**

   a. artificial

   b. rampant

   c. arguable

   d. traditional

   e. certain

4 **Which is not listed as a possible health hazard in the passage?**

   a. spraying chemicals and pesticides on crops

   b. the placement of natural enemies of pests

   c. the injection of artificial hormones into livestock

   d. toxic pesticides that destroy soil and water quality

   e. manipulation of genes of grains, fruits, and vegetables

5 **What is the author's attitude toward organic farming?**

   a. critical

   b. positive

   c. indifferent

   d. skeptical

   e. neutral

Economic Viability of Organic Farming

Pre-reading Activity

True or false?

1. Organic food is less expensive than non-organic.	TRUE	FALSE
2. Organic farming requires more space than non-organic.	TRUE	FALSE
3. More chemicals are used in organic farming.	TRUE	FALSE

Grocery shoppers have clearly noticed that organic food is pricier than food grown by traditional methods. They probably believe that they are paying for healthier food of higher quality. While it is becoming more evident that organic food is healthier than other food, it is also clear that the production methods are certainly more expensive. 5

Using the same soil annually for crop production can <u>leach</u> the soil of its nutrients, so farmers often use artificial methods of enriching the soil with nitrates. Organic farmers commonly use crop rotation and allow the ground to lie for some period of time to help the soil recover its nutrient content. Also, organic farmers commonly enrich the soil with manure or compost, which is more expensive to 10 transport.

These unique ways to avoid using artificial farming also take up space. For example, caged chickens are less expensive to raise than free-range chickens. Farmers can maximize productivity of a physical space by confining hens that never leave their cages in extremely close quarters while feeding them manufactured 15 feed. However, free-range chickens lay eggs that contain many nutrients that their cage-produced counterparts do not. This is a result of allowing free-range chickens to pick food from the soil that contains algae, which is healthy for humans when delivered in the form of eggs.

The amount of land that organic farming requires makes it impossible to apply 20 to the entire food production system. Organic farming results in lower yields with a comparative large amount of land, so this can affect the environment negatively in an indirect way. The question of organic farming and its benefit still remains, and more research and innovation is clearly needed. 25

Reading Tips

prefix "en-"

to make a person or thing be in a particular state

enable
enlarge
enrich
ensure
endanger
enslave
entrust
encourage
endear

1 **What is the passage mainly about?**

a. the pros and cons of organic farming
b. the negative aspects of organic farming
c. different methods of making soil fertile
d. the science behind organic farming methods
e. the benefits of crop production in organic farming

2 **Which is closest in meaning to the word "leach"?**

a. alter
b. cultivate
c. devastate
d. deplete
e. pacify

3 **Which of the following is NOT true about free-range chickens?**

a. They lay eggs that are rich in nutrition.
b. They are expensive to raise and care for.
c. They require less physical space than caged chickens.
d. They are not kept in close quarters like caged chickens.
e. Raising free-range chickens is less productive than raising caged chickens.

4 **What is the author's attitude toward organic farming?**

a. It is going to pose a threat to the environment.
b. It is simply a trend that will pass in the near future.
c. It is promising, but more work and study need to be done.
d. It will completely replace traditional farming in the future.
e. It is just too expensive and requires too much work to be viable.

5 **Why do organic farmers allow the soil to have a period of dormancy between crop rotation?**

_____

A Words

A1. Fill in the blank according to the definition.

profitability	advocate	confine	manufacture	manure

1 _____: to speak in favor of somebody or of a plan

2 _____: solid waste from farm animals used on crops to help them grow

3 _____: the degree to which something is producing a profit or useful result

4 _____: to make goods or materials, usually in large quantities in a factory

5 _____: to restrict someone's movement; to keep an animal in a closed space

A2. Choose the most appropriate word for each blank.

1 Foods produced from cow's milk are defined as dairy _____.
   a. cheese   b. calcium   c. produce   d. energy

2 David _____ the saddle on his bike to make it more comfortable.
   a. adhered   b. modified   c. lessened   d. challenged

3 Dozens of trucks were used to _____ relief items to the earthquake victims.
   a. transport   b. transact   c. translate   d. transform

4 Many volunteers joined the campaign to _____ illiteracy in the country.
   a. choose   b. contain   c. include   d. eliminate

5 The _____ of the couch feels like genuine leather, but it is really artificial leather.
   a. density   b. fitness   c. quantity   d. texture

A3. Complete each sentence with one of the words from the box.

environmental	counterpart	benefit	hormones	minute

1 We have to work together for our mutual _____.

2 The release of _____ in the body sends messages to other cells.

3 The Indian leader and his Pakistani _____ will hold talks next month.

4 You almost could not tell, but there were _____ traces of poison in it.

5 Companies that do not have _____ policies cannot receive government funding.

B Expressions and Phrases

B1. Fill in the blank using an expression from the box.

a large amount of	in response to	so that	in the form of

1   This site has _____ information on the Korean War.
2   I had to slow down _____ he could catch up with my car.
3   The sign for the staircase to the banquet room was _____ a big 'S.'
4   _____ consumers' complaints, the company is reviewing the safety of the product.

B2. Complete each sentence with an expression from the reading passages.
   (Change the form of the verb if necessary.)

do harm	be attracted to	pay for	result in

1   Many tourists _____ the natural beauty of the Alps.
2   You don't have to _____ the concert tickets in advance.
3   A wrong decision now can _____ problems later in your life.
4   A vaccine which has not been properly tested may _____ to many people.

C Summary

Complete the summary with the appropriate words and expressions.

yield	traditional	nutritious	expensive
demanding	alternative	innovation	healthier

Organic farming is growing in response to _____ farming methods that are unhealthy. The market is _____ healthier options. Organic farming uses _____ methods instead of using chemical sprays. Though organic options are more _____ and labor-intensive, they are growing in popularity.

Organic food is _____ than non-organic. However, the production methods which organic farmers use, such as crop rotation, are still very pricy to grow products. But it gives us highly _____ food. One thing that is clear is that more research and _____ is needed for organic farming to _____ large-scale results truly.

MIND TRICKS

Absent-Minded Genius

meeting @ 9:00 am

Pre-reading Activity

Read the list of words below quickly. Cover them. Then write as many as you can remember in order.
picture – statue – chair – sink – shoe – water – mango – candle – fan – computer

_____ _____ _____ _____ _____
_____ _____ _____ _____ _____

Tatiana Cooley who won the US memory championship in 1999 has been given many titles. One of them is "The World's Smartest Beauty." The other is "The World's Greatest Memorizer." Tatiana memorizes 100 faces and <u>corresponding</u> names in a few minutes. She can memorize a string of 4,000 numbers in a row as fast as she can read them. Or let her read 500 words in a row. Then, she will repeat them back to you in perfect order.

One of many other titles that her friends and family call her is "The World's Most Absent-minded Woman."   (A)   Tatiana can perform fabulous memory feats on stage for crowds to see, she cannot remember things in daily life. That is why many call her "The Post-it Queen." She carries around Post-it notes to jot down notes about things she must remember to do, people she must call, and reminders of   (B)   she put her personal belongings. "She forgets everything, everything, everything," says her mom. Tatiana forgets to show up for appointments and cannot remember what time they are. She says if she does not write all of her appointments on Post-it notes, she would never remember to show up for anything.

Tatiana explains that memorization and remembering daily tasks are different skills. Memorizing is about visualizing things. For example, when memorizing a list of 500 words, she makes mental images of each and every one of the 500 words and then connects the words and their images together. Once they are strongly connected through these mental images, they are easy to remember. She explains that the world's best memorizers spend their time in their imagination, and that is why they have trouble remembering earthly tasks.

1

5

10

15

20

Reading Tips

usage of "order"

noun

1. the disposition of things arranged in relation to each other
   The books are placed in alphabetical order.

2. a direction or instruction that is given by someone in authority
   I was given a direct order by the President.

3. a situation in which law or established authority are obeyed
   The police were called in to maintain order.

1　**What is the passage mainly about?**

a. Tatiana's awesome memory feats and her forgetfulness

b. the way of memorizing a string of 4,000 numbers

c. Tatiana's useful techniques for memorizing

d. Tatiana Cooley's life and her success story

e. smart Post-it notes helping Tatiana

2　**Which is closest in meaning to the word "corresponding"?**

a. executive

b. expected

c. consistent

d. dissimilar

e. matching

3　**Which best fits in the blanks?**

(A)		(B)
a. Since	⋯	whom
b. Because	⋯	what
c. Although	⋯	that
d. While	⋯	where
e. As	⋯	which

4　**Which of the following is NOT true about Tatiana Cooley?**

a. She takes Post-it notes everywhere with her.

b. She keeps daily to-do lists not to forget things.

c. She has no interest in the people and things around her.

d. She took first prize in the US memory championship in 1999.

e. She has two techniques for memorizing: visualization and association.

5　**Why does Tatiana have trouble remembering daily tasks?**

_____

Tricks of the Mind

Pre-reading Activity

1. Have you ever been hypnotized?
2. Have you ever seen hypnosis done in movies or on TV?
3. Do you know anyone who has been hypnotized?

Derren Brown is a star in the UK because of several shows he made between 2000 and present day. These shows have aired on the BBC and helped make Derren a superstar in Britain. Derren started off as a stage hypnotist. This means that he did a show where he picked out audience members, brought them up on the stage, and hypnotized them to do strange things. For example, he will say "Relax, relax, and follow everything I say." The person will then enter sort of a trance and do whatever Derren says. Often he will say, "When I count to three, you will be five years old again." After uttering "One, two, three," the adult will suddenly start talking like he/she did when he/she was five and begin running around the room playing with everything.

This is the power of hypnosis. Certain people can be hypnotized to do almost anything. These kinds of people are the people that advertising companies love. When these people watch TV, commercials get inside their heads with ease. Derren knows how to make his shows successful, and he can also find people who are easy to manipulate. In some of his shows, Derren demonstrates how easy it is to hypnotize people with just a word or two.

Derren says that he uses a variety of methods to achieve his illusions including traditional magic techniques, memory techniques, hypnosis, body language reading, and cognitive psychology. Using his knowledge and skill, he appears to be able to <u>predict</u> and influence people's thoughts and read the subtle physical signs that _____ what a person is thinking.

Some people question his abilities saying he uses actors or stooges in his show. But Derren claims to have never used <u>them</u> in his work. Can you believe that he has this fantastic talent?

Reading Tips

suffix "-ology"

to refer to a particular branch of knowledge

biology
geology
zoology
ecology
astrology
sociology
mythology
psychology
anthropology
paleontology

1   **What is the passage mainly about?**

   a. Derren Brown and his trickery
   b. the power of stage hypnotists
   c. Derren Brown and his abilities
   d. hypnosis and cognitive psychology
   e. how to manipulate ordinary people

2   **Which is closest in meaning to the word "predict"?**

   a. fulfill
   b. neglect
   c. foresee
   d. clarify
   e. alert

3   **Which best fits in the blank?**

   a. trick
   b. indicate
   c. manage
   d. instruct
   e. treat

4   **What can be inferred from the passage?**

   a. Most people cannot be easily hypnotized.
   b. Derren is going to retire soon from his shows.
   c. Almost all people can probably be hypnotized.
   d. People like to be hypnotized when they watch TV.
   e. Certain kinds of people are more easily manipulated than others.

5   **What does the word "them" refer to?**

_____

A   Words

A1. Fill in the blank according to the definition.

appointment	utter	memorize	illusion	earthly

1 _____ : a meeting set for a particular place and time

2 _____ : relating to life on earth rather than to heaven

3 _____ : to learn by heart; to commit something to memory

4 _____ : to produce an audible expression with your voice

5 _____ : something that deceives you by producing a misleading view of reality

A2. Choose the most appropriate word for each blank.

1 It can't be _____ that he is one of the most reputable authors.
   a. questioned   b. investigated   c. replied   d. exploited

2 Playing with blocks helps the _____ development of children.
   a. excessive   b. mental   c. renowned   d. specific

3 Many people have suspected that China has _____ its currency.
   a. destroyed   b. visualized   c. manipulated   d. demonstrated

4 People under _____ frequently recall forgotten events in the past.
   a. attack   b. hypnosis   c. pension   d. fate

5 There are some scientists who _____ a rise in sea levels by 2 meters by 2085.
   a. exposure   b. enhance   c. predict   d. prolong

A3. Complete each sentence with one of the words from the box.

belongings	audience	imagination	influence	cognitive

1 Somebody left his/her _____ in the locker room.

2 It's clearly evident that stress impairs some _____ functions.

3 Allowing children to use their _____ is important in education.

4 The masters of the Renaissance had a big _____ on my artwork.

5 The _____ was shocked when the lion turned to his trainer and bit his leg.

B Expressions and Phrases

B1. Fill in the blank using an expression from the box.

in a row	for anything	each and every	a variety of

1 I wouldn't give up the chance to meet Park Ji-sung _____.
2 The Chicago Bulls won the NBA championship three times _____.
3 As promised, _____ one of you will receive two free tickets to the concert.
4 These shirts have just arrived in time for spring. They come in _____ colors and patterns.

B2. Complete each sentence with an expression from the reading passages.
   (Change the form of the verb if necessary.)

jot down	show up	pick out	start off

1 Ron waited and waited in the pouring rain, but she never _____.
2 Please _____ your phone number and email address, or I'll forget them.
3 I won't let my mom _____ my clothes—my friends will make fun of me.
4 My brother who won the Pitcher of the Year actually _____ as an outfielder.

C Summary

Complete the summary with the appropriate words and expressions.

single	tasks	manipulate	remember
hypnotizing	skeptics	connections	Memorizer

Tatiana Cooley is called many things—one of them is the World's Greatest _____. She can _____ 100 faces and names in minutes. She says memorizing is not that difficult when you visualize things and find the _____ between them. Ironically, Tatiana is also called the Post-it Queen because she cannot remember simple everyday _____.

Derren Brown is famous in the UK for several TV shows. Starting off as a hypnotist, Derren soon realized he was quite good at _____ people. On his shows, Derren looks for people who are easy to _____. Some of these people can be hypnotized with a _____ word. While Brown says he does not use actors or stooges, there are _____.

THE WORLD OF ART

Viral Art

Pre-reading Activity

Match the artists and their masterpieces.

| ⓐ Scream | ⓑ Mona Lisa | ⓒ Starry Night | ⓓ Girl with a Pearl Earring |

1. Johannes Vermeer _____
2. Edvard Munch _____
3. Leonardo da Vinci _____
4. Vincent van Gogh _____

Art is everywhere—from the 18-month-old toddler who spreads ketchup all over some paper to the masters like Leonardo da Vinci and Michelangelo. Today, a new artist from Great Britain is making headlines with his glass art. This glass art, beautiful as it may be, has a bit of a deadly twist to it.

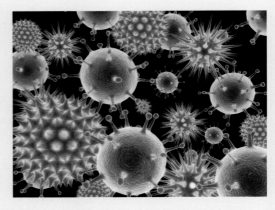

The sculptor, Luke Jerram, has spent years learning about deadly viruses such as HIV, smallpox, and the more recent H1N1 virus—more commonly known as the swine flu virus. For over five years, he has studied these ___(A)___ killers and is now having them blown in glass. The response to this new art form has been amazing. Beautifully rendered in milky glass, the nasty viruses shimmer like crystal on mirrored surfaces. These transparent, fragile-looking spheres are actually the greatest killers in human history.

Jerram became interested in the viruses after seeing illustrations of these deadly subjects on TV and in a variety of magazine articles. His discovery path was interesting. He learned viruses are so small that even electron microscopes cannot make out all of their details. He noticed that if he made these viruses one million times bigger, people could better understand or at least <u>appreciate</u> them better.

Jerram wants people to see these little critters and better understand the impact they have on humanity. For something so small to kill so many people each year is truly mind-boggling. Jerram wants us to think about that. During his research, Jerram finds out that even virologists do not fully ___(B)___ many aspects of viruses and how they work. He hopes we can find out the answers to many of these questions. He hopes his artwork helps people learn more about these enemies. More importantly, he hopes to inspire future scientists who may be the ones to find cures for these deadly bugs.

1
5
10
15
20
25

Reading Tips

usage of "may"

1. used to indicate possibility
   It may snow tomorrow.
2. used to indicate permission or opportunity
   You may kiss the bride.
3. used to indicate contingency
   I may be wrong but I really think I should take the offer.
4. used to express hopes and wishes
   May she rest in peace.

1   **What is the passage mainly about?**

a. an appreciation of the Viral Art
b. severe impacts of deadly viruses
c. creating a new art form by using viruses
d. Luke Jerram and his mind-boggling life
e. a creative painter and his inspiring artwork

2   **Why does the author mention "Art is everywhere"?**

a. to explain that art is difficult
b. to tell that anything can be a work of art
c. to tell that we can find artists everywhere
d. to explain that art is difficult to understand
e. to insist that artworks can be placed everywhere

3   **Which is closest in meaning to the word "appreciate"?**

a. satisfy
b. disregard
c. comprehend
d. accomplish
e. assign

4   **Which best fits in the blanks?**

	(A)		(B)
a.	small	⋯	prescribe
b.	huge	⋯	criticize
c.	enough	⋯	estimate
d.	tiny	⋯	understand
e.	micro	⋯	diagnose

5   **Which of the following is NOT true about Luke Jerram?**

a. He enlarges the shapes of viruses by using glass.
b. He wants people to appreciate these deadly viruses.
c. His new form of art has been underestimated by people.
d. He wants scientists to find cures to deadly viruses in the future.
e. He thinks people should understand the viruses' impact on humanity.

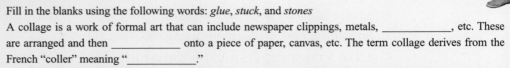

Art Collage

Pre-reading Activity

Fill in the blanks using the following words: *glue*, *stuck*, and *stones*

A collage is a work of formal art that can include newspaper clippings, metals, _____, etc. These are arranged and then _____ onto a piece of paper, canvas, etc. The term collage derives from the French "coller" meaning "_____."

Anyone who has ever taken an art class in school is sure to be familiar with collage art. It is one of the most popular art projects with students around the world not only because it is fun to do but also because anyone can do it. Like it or not, the art form known as collage is making a comeback. This comeback is not just for kindergarten to twelfth grade students in public and private schools. Adult learning centers are offering these creative classes to everyone from young adults to some of the oldest senior citizens alive today.

To make an exciting collage, all you need is a bunch of different materials, some glue, and a surface such as pieces of paper, wood panels, or canvases. The materials might include anything from clippings from newspapers and magazines, to photographs, to pieces of cloth, rope, or string. One's creativity is the only restriction to what kind of materials can find their way onto a collage.

Once you have all of these things, you can begin to assemble or construct your collage. One method is to paste all of your materials onto a plain surface to create pictures or designs that are truly your own. The right adhesive is very important for creating a long-lasting masterpiece. An <u>inferior</u> glue will only last so long before you start finding pieces of your collage on the living room floor!

Another approach to making a collage is to glue your materials onto a painting or drawing you have already created. In this way, you can use your materials to complete your picture giving it a three-dimensional effect or an added texture. Whichever way you choose, collages are fun because whatever you decide to make is entirely up to you and your own imagination!

1

5

10

15

20

25

Reading Tips

types of visual art

collage
comics
drawing
graffiti
illustration
painting
photography
etching
lithography
sculpture

1   **What is the first paragraph mainly about?**

a. collage art and its creative process

b. the materials needed to make collages

c. the resurgence of the art form known as collage

d. using your imagination to create great collage art

e. how to assemble collage art with various materials

2   **Which is closest in meaning to the word "inferior"?**

a. superior

b. expensive

c. substandard

d. detailed

e. typical

3   **Which of the following is NOT true?**

a. A great piece of collage art needs proper adhesive.

b. You can use any materials you like on your own collage.

c. You can start a collage by gluing materials onto a blank surface.

d. Most people are not familiar with the art form known as collage.

e. Today, people of all ages can have a chance to make collage art.

4   **Which best fits in the blanks?**

> Collage is a visual art which can be created by assembling a set of _____ such as newspapers, photographs, cloths, rope, etc. The material you want to put on a plain surface can vary widely depending on your _____.

a. materials, idea

b. brushes, staff

c. contents, clothes

d. connections, independence

e. features, picture

5   **What does the author say is the thing that limits what to put on a collage?**

_____

A Words

A1. Fill in the blank according to the definition.

toddler	cure	assemble	inferior	master

1 _____: a person who is very skilled at something
2 _____: to put or fit together the parts of something
3 _____: poor in quality or lower in rank, degree, or grade
4 _____: a medicine or medical treatment used to restore health
5 _____: a very young child, usually at the age of learning to walk

A2. Choose the most appropriate word for each blank.

1 Please help me _____ these stamps at the bottom of the form.
   a. create   b. issue   c. paste   d. print

2 _____ and other sealants are so important to engineers and architects.
   a. Adhesives   b. Fluids   c. Liquids   d. Toxins

3 Sometimes locust swarms _____ out over large areas and destroy everything.
   a. figured   b. spread   c. compressed   d. discovered

4 Global climate change will ultimately have dire effects on _____.
   a. appreciation   b. conclusion   c. humanity   d. purpose

5 His irresponsible speech provoked an angry _____ from the citizens.
   a. customer   b. response   c. stimulation   d. output

A3. Complete each sentence with one of the words from the box.

restrictions	virologist	creativity	microscope	masterpieces

1 Being curious and observant will help enhance your _____.
2 I always wanted to get a _____ to look at the world of the small.
3 As in its name, a _____ studies the structure and functions of viruses.
4 The fascinating painting counts as one of the greatest _____ of the century.
5 The US imposed many flight _____ after the attacks of September 11, 2001.

B Expressions and Phrases

B1. Fill in the blank using an expression from the box.

at least	such as	a bunch of	like it or not

1 _____, you have to accept the fact that she declined your proposal.

2 You should exercise _____ 20 minutes every other day, or every day.

3 The disease involves physical symptoms _____ dizziness and headaches.

4 To make fresh lemonade, you only need _____ lemons, water, and sugar.

B2. Complete each sentence with an expression from the reading passages.
(Change the form of the verb if necessary.)

make headlines	make out	be familiar with	be up to

1 It _____ you whether you choose to take the risk or not.

2 Are you totally positive that you _____ the safety procedures?

3 The shocking incident has _____ throughout the world for weeks.

4 I couldn't _____ what she was saying because she was mumbling a lot.

C Summary

Complete the summary with the appropriate words and expressions.

deadliest	comeback	sculptor	pasting
understand	artwork	imaginations	limitation

Luke Jerram, a creative artist, is a(n) _____ of glass art. Jerram is blowing glass art of some of the world's _____ viruses. He believes if people can see these tiny creatures, they may better _____ the tiny killers. Jerram hopes his _____ will inspire future scientists to find a cure for these deadly bugs.

Collage art is making a(n) _____. From kindergartens to adult learning centers, it is being used to help people share their _____. A variety of materials can be used to create this art form. The only _____ is your creativity. Also, keep in mind—the proper adhesive is an important part for _____ all the parts and pieces of a new masterpiece.

PEOPLE AND ANIMALS

Snakes: A Good Story

Pre-reading Activity

True or false?
1. Living snakes are found on every continent except Antarctica.   TRUE   FALSE
2. A king cobra is a large, powerful snake, and we can see it only in India.   TRUE   FALSE
3. A boa constrictor is the world's longest venomous snake.   TRUE   FALSE

Daniel Greene is an epileptic. Epilepsy is a disorder of the brain that results   1
in convulsions or seizures. If a person with epilepsy knows in advance that he/
she will have a seizure, he/she can get to a place of safety and sit down. This is
very important because if the person has the seizure on a busy street, it can be
dangerous.   5

A few people with this disability have a seizure-alert dog. It takes two years
for seizure-alert dogs to be trained, and there are not many available. Some people
have waited for a decade to receive one. The specially-trained dog can feel the
changes in a person's body and alert him/her that a seizure is <u>forthcoming</u>. Then
that person can get to a safe place.   10

Daniel Greene did not want to wait for a seizure-alert dog. He knew that his
pet python, a nearly 5-foot boa constrictor, could do the same job. He couldn't
explain how the python knew he had a seizure coming on. (1) When Daniel was
sitting around watching TV with his pet python wrapped around his neck one day,
the python squeezed Daniel a few minutes before a seizure occurred. Thereafter he   15
started taking it everywhere he went. (2) He took him to the bank, the post office,
and the grocery store—everywhere.

(3) When Daniel walked into any establishment, managers or workers would
yell at him, "You can't bring that python in here! Get out of here!" He noticed that
many people in public were uncomfortable
when they saw his pet.

(4) Daniel and his lawyer proved that
the python could perform the same task as a
seizure-alert dog. As a result, his python can
accompany him wherever he goes. (5) If you
ever see a man driving down the road with
a python around his neck, that is probably
Daniel and his pet python "Redrock."

Reading Tips

usage of "hyphen(-)"

a punctuation mark used to
connect the parts of a compound
word or to separate syllables of a
single word

1. used in adjectives formed from
two or more words
a 50-year-old judge

2. used with the adverb when used
adjectivally with another word
well-established principles

3. used to avoid ambiguities
a little-used car / a little used-car

1 **What is the passage mainly about?**

a. a rise of seizure-alert dogs in the world
b. a specially-trained python for the epileptic
c. a disorder called epilepsy and how it functions in everyday life
d. an amazing story of Daniel Greene and his seizure-alert python
e. a relationship between the disabled and seizure-alert animals

2 **Which is closest in meaning to the word "forthcoming"?**

a. gone
b. distant
c. inevitable
d. escapable
e. approaching

3 **What can be inferred from the passage?**

a. Daniel trained the snake to take it with him in public.
b. People think it is very cool to have a seizure-alert animal.
c. People do not like to be around any kind of assistance animal.
d. People suffering from epilepsy can easily get a seizure-alert dog.
e. People may be more comfortable with seizure-alert dogs than snakes.

4 **Where does the following sentence fit best?**

> However, there was one problem taking his pet into public settings.

a. (1)   b. (2)   c. (3)   d. (4)   e. (5)

5 **How does the python alert Daniel to an upcoming seizure?**

_____

The Sanctuary

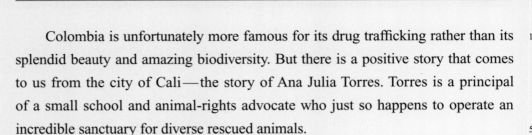

Pre-reading Activity

Did you know?
An animal sanctuary is a facility where animals are brought to live and be protected until their natural death. Unlike a zoo, a sanctuary is not open to the public, and its important mission, beyond caring for animals, is educating the public about animals.

Colombia is unfortunately more famous for its drug trafficking rather than its splendid beauty and amazing biodiversity. But there is a positive story that comes to us from the city of Cali—the story of Ana Julia Torres. Torres is a principal of a small school and animal-rights advocate who just so happens to operate an incredible sanctuary for diverse rescued animals. [5]

The sanctuary that Torres runs for over 800 animals is ironically linked to the drug business. Most of the animals that she takes in and cares for come from many of the local drug traffickers. When some of the drug lords are arrested or murdered, they leave behind a host of animals—from big African lions to pygmy marmosets. One of the first calls that the police make is to Torres to request that she take in the [10] animals.

Torres' sanctuary also gets other critters coming from people who are caught trying to smuggle animals. This is because Colombia's biodiversity is astonishing, and many people make a <u>lucrative</u> living by sneaking animals in and out of the country. Animals that have been seized are King Vultures, toucans, spider monkeys, [15] caimans, and even cougars. All these animals get to live out the remaining part of their lives at the sanctuary. They do not have to worry about humans trying to exploit them for profit.

Torres receives help from the Cali environmental police and private donors, but she does not take funds from the Colombian government. While there are other [20] animal-rights advocates in the area that are concerned about the growth of the sanctuary, <u>they</u> still support it. _____, one day, Colombia can move beyond its current infamy and become famous for its wildlife and animal sanctuaries. [25]

phrasal verbs with "live"

live for: to consider something as the most important thing in your life
I live for the movies.

live out: to continue to live in a particular way or place until one's death
They lived out the rest of their lives with dignity.

live off: to get your income or food from somebody or something
You shouldn't live off your parents!

live on: to continue to exist; to eat a particular type of food a lot
Even though he is no longer with us, his music lives on.
They live on rice and beans.

1 **What is the passage mainly about?**

a. the biodiversity and beauty of Colombia

b. the animal sanctuary run by Ana Julia Torres

c. the side effects of the Colombian drug business

d. the animals that people try to smuggle out of Colombia

e. the Colombian government with an indifferent attitude to the sanctuary

2 **Which is closest in meaning to the word "lucrative"?**

a. decent

b. fruitless

c. profitable

d. adequate

e. unproductive

3 **Which best fits in the blank?**

a. Instead

b. Hopefully

c. Therefore

d. Sincerely

e. Unfortunately

4 **Which of the following is NOT true?**

a. People smuggle animals to make money in Colombia.

b. Torres' sanctuary protects rescued animals until they die.

c. Torres uses her school as a sanctuary for rescued animals.

d. We can see many different kinds of animals in Torres' sanctuary.

e. Torres' sanctuary is a place where animals can be taken care of.

5 **What does the word "they" refer to?**

_____

A Words

A1. Fill in the blank according to the definition.

astonishing	infamy	request	sanctuary	seizure

1 _____: a sudden attack of illness

2 _____: causing amazement or surprise

3 _____: a reputation for something bad or evil

4 _____: an act of asking for something in a formal way

5 _____: a tract of land where animals can live and be safe

A2. Choose the most appropriate word for each blank.

1 During a(n) _____, the clothing around the neck needs to be loosened.
   a. convulsion   b. turbulence   c. expansion   d. comprehension

2 The team just signed a(n) _____ contract with the star basketball player.
   a. indifferent   b. uncomfortable   c. lucrative   d. humble

3 When it gets cold, grandma always _____ one of her blankets around me.
   a. wraps   b. fastens   c. camouflages   d. occurs

4 His _____ new book is being released a little later than originally planned.
   a. remaining   b. forthcoming   c. sneaking   d. tiresome

5 Before starting the US 'wet foot dry foot' policy, Cubans were _____ into the U.S.A. by boats.
   a. rescued   b. squeezed   c. disclosed   d. smuggled

A3. Complete each sentence with one of the words from the box.

exploit	biodiversity	donor	splendid	ironically

1 Many countries rushed to Africa to _____ its natural resources.

2 _____, my daughter's cough got even worse after taking the medicine.

3 The Palace of Versailles in Paris was more _____ than I had dreamed.

4 A loss of the earth's _____ could lead to larger problems for the global ecosystem.

5 The owner of the restaurant was the biggest _____ at the fundraiser last night.

B Expressions and Phrases

B1. Fill in the blank using an expression from the box.

rather than	in advance	one day	thereafter

1 My landlord asked me to pay a month's rent _____.

2 He encourages his son to pursue happiness _____ money.

3 Jennifer emigrated to Australia, and _____ I haven't met her.

4 It is our sincerest hope that _____ we will not have people living in poverty.

B2. Complete each sentence with an expression from the reading passages.
(Change the form of the verb if necessary.)

worry about	care for	be linked to	get out of

1 We have to pack and _____ here before the volcano erupts.

2 Rachel will be _____ my puppy until I get back from Tokyo next week.

3 Jane is _____ her brother who has been hospitalized after a car accident.

4 Exposure to ultraviolet rays _____ skin cancer. Don't forget to wear your sunscreen.

C Summary

Complete the summary with the appropriate words and expressions.

seizures	rescued	python	infamous
principal	epilepsy	shelter	everywhere

Daniel Greene suffers from epilepsy which is a disorder that results in _____.
While there are some seizure-alert dogs to help people with _____, Daniel has
another helping animal—a snake. Many didn't allow the _____ inside their
establishments. Daniel showed that his python could perform the same task as seizure-alert
dogs do, and now Daniel's python goes _____ with him.

While Colombia is _____ for its drug trafficking, there is also good news
coming out of this beautiful country. Julia Torres is a school _____ who
has operated a sanctuary for _____ lions, monkeys, birds, and more. Torres
receives help from the environmental police and private donors to _____
rescued animals in Colombia.

EMERGING JOBS IN THE 21ST CENTURY

What about Becoming a Zoologist?

Pre-reading Activity

Fill in the blanks using the following words: *habitats*, *zoos*, and *aspects*

Zoologists are scientists studying all _____ of animal life, including their habitats, anatomy, life histories, and physiology. They study animals in a laboratory and in their natural _____, and they also work at _____.

Zoologists are scientists who study how animals live and how they adapt to their environment in a laboratory and in their natural habitat. By studying animals closely, (1) they can classify them and understand how (2) they function as individuals or as members of populations and communities. (3) They also study creatures such as reptiles and amphibians. Sometimes (4) they must catch them, tranquilize them, and take them to the vet to test the health of these creatures. Then, (5) they return them to the wild.

Zoologists may hear that the Canadian wolves are endangered. To find out if this is true and how close to extinction the wolves are, they must do some ground research. Zoologists know what territories the wolves live in, where and how they sleep, how many wolves are in a pack, and what they eat. Armed with this information, the zoologist will pack up his/her belongings and go into the territories where these endangered wolves live. He/She will find their dens and count how many wolves are in the dens. The zoologist will check their habitats to make sure there is enough food in their surroundings. Then, the zoologist will check if there is any construction or other destruction in the area that would threaten the wolves.

After doing this field research, the zoologist will return to the office to write long reports and recommendations on the status of the wolves. It is not an easy job. A zoologist must be well-studied on the habitats and nature of wolves, both to find them and to protect himself/herself from the wolves _____.

You can also find zoologists working in natural history museums, zoos, research laboratories, and national parks. Many teach in colleges or work as environmental consultants. If you want to be a zoologist, you should enjoy synthesizing information. You also need to be patient, well organized, and alert since the work involves keeping track of research, handling huge amounts of data, and being exposed to unpredictable animal behavior.

1
5
10
15
20
25

Reading Tips

classification of animals

mammal: a warm-blooded animal that has more or less hair on the body and nourishes the young with milk

bird: a warm-blooded, egg-laying animal with forelimbs modified into wings, feathers, scaly legs, and a beak that can usually fly

reptile: a cold-blooded, usually egg-laying animal having scales or horny plates on the skin

amphibian: a cold-blooded animal that can live both on land and in water

fish: a cold-blooded, aquatic animal that is covered with scales and usually has gills and fins

1 **What is the passage mainly about?**

   a. the dangers of becoming a zoologist

   b. the general job description of a zoologist

   c. the way that a zoologist studies Canadian wolves

   d. the different animals that a zoologist has to study

   e. the academic background needed to be a zoologist

2 **Which is closest in meaning to the word "tranquilize"?**

   a. count on

   b. hand in

   c. wipe out

   d. clear up

   e. calm down

3 **Choose the underlined "they" which refers to a different noun.**

   a. (1)   b. (2)   c. (3)   d. (4)   e. (5)

4 **Which best fits in the blank?**

   a. if a vet is needed

   b. if an encounter occurs

   c. if they breed more often

   d. if they go completely extinct

   e. if they get scared of a stranger

5 **What can be inferred from the passage?**

   a. Zoologists always work in the field.

   b. Zoologists primarily focus on the study of reptiles.

   c. Zoologists do not do ground research out in the wild.

   d. Endangered animals are closely watched by zoologists.

   e. Zoologists are able to predict every aspect of animal behavior.

EMERGING JOBS IN THE 21ST CENTURY
Predicting the Future & Future Jobs

Pre-reading Activity

Look at the title of the passage, and write down five words you think will be in the passage.

_____ _____ _____ _____ _____

Now scan the passage, and see if you were right. How many? _____

The future is unpredictable, but that does not stop futurists from doing the best they can to figure out what the future will look like. Let's look at some quotes from people over the past century or so that had trouble foretelling the future. 1

In 1977, Ken Olsen, the chairman of Digital Equipment Corporation said, *"There is no reason why anyone would want a computer in their home."* Going 5 further back in time, the president of the Michigan Savings Bank, while talking to Henry Ford's lawyer about investing in Ford Motor Company, said, *"The horse is here to stay, but the automobile is only a novelty, a fad."* Here's another one. Back in 1878, the head of the British Royal Mail said, *"The Americans need the telephone, but we do not. We have plenty of messenger boys."* 10

As you can clearly see, _____. Sometimes we are so wrong in our predictions. If the gentlemen <u>quoted</u> above had been correct, we would not have had millions of computer programmers, engineers, designers, operators, electricians, just to name a few. So, what does the future look like for some science and technology jobs? The folks at Future Savvy work hard to try and accurately 15 predict what the future holds and what kind of jobs will be in demand.

Some interesting jobs that they predict will be available between 2020 and 2030 are:

- Body Part Maker—creation of human body parts such as organs and limbs is going to happen. We will need the makers, the stores, and even the repair shops.
- Space Pilot, Architect, and Tour Guide—with space tourism in its infancy, it will undoubtedly blossom, and the need for pilots, space architects, and tour guides is obvious.

Explore some links on future jobs and see which one sounds exciting for you!

1   **What is the second paragraph mainly about?**

   a. futurists and their predictions
   b. the future and its unpredictability
   c. several interesting jobs of the future
   d. space tourism and its uncertain future
   e. examples of incorrect predictions people made

2   **Which best fits in the blank?**

   a. no one is perfect
   b. haste makes waste
   c. we need fortune-tellers
   d. people do not believe their destiny
   e. the British don't have telephones

3   **Which is closest in meaning to the word "quoted"?**

   a. cited
   b. classified
   c. separated
   d. subtitled
   e. criticized

4   **Which of the following is NOT true?**

   a. A futurists' job is to predict the future.
   b. It's not easy to predict what will happen in the future.
   c. More people will be traveling into space in the future.
   d. Telephones had come into wide use in the late of 1870.
   e. All the gentlemen's prediction quoted in the passage were wrong.

5   **Why does the author mention that space pilots can be a future job?**

   _____

A Words

A1. Fill in the blank according to the definition.

laboratory	tranquilize	synthesize	prediction	blossom

1 _____: to develop; to grow in quality or quantity

2 _____: an act of stating what you think will happen

3 _____: to sedate by administering a drug, usually to an animal

4 _____: a room or building used to conduct scientific experiments

5 _____: to form by combining parts or elements to make a new whole

A2. Choose the most appropriate word for each blank.

1 The _____ caused by the typhoon cost the country a billion dollars.
   a. demonstration   b. replacement   c. examination   d. destruction

2 The big game between the Yankees and the Mets is completely _____.
   a. fashionable   b. natural   c. unpredictable   d. correct

3 The homeowner felt _____ by the young boys when they banged on her door.
   a. threatened   b. guilty   c. progressive   d. exposed

4 More and more creatures are joining the _____ list every day as habitats dwindle.
   a. territorial   b. independent   c. practical   d. endangered

5 Most scientists agree that the _____ of the dinosaurs happened 65 million years ago.
   a. disclosure   b. emission   c. rejection   d. extinction

A3. Complete each sentence with one of the words from the box.

amphibians	organ	novelty	corporations	architect

1 In tourist areas, you can buy some unique _____ items in most stores.

2 Since she was five, she has wanted to be a(n) _____ and create buildings.

3 You may be surprised to learn that the largest _____ of our body is the skin.

4 The protestors are trying to get the multinational _____ to pay higher wages.

5 It is amazing how _____ start life with gills then develop lungs in adulthood.

B Expressions and Phrases

B1. Fill in the blank using an expression from the box.

to name a few	in demand	in its infancy	or so

1 Daily disposable contact lenses are _____ these days.

2 The study of the cosmos and the Big Bang is still _____.

3 My sister had a baby girl after she had been in labor for 14 hours _____.

4 We have a huge range of household items—furniture, refrigerators, vacuum cleaners, _____.

B2. Complete each sentence with an expression from the reading passages.
    (Change the form of the verb if necessary.)

be armed with	make sure	pack up	be here to stay

1 James asked his brother to come by the lab and _____ his stuff.

2 Everyone, we need to _____ that all the students are on the bus.

3 It's obvious that online shopping _____ whether you like it or not.

4 All evolutionary biologists need to _____ the basics of Darwin's research.

C Summary

Complete the summary with the appropriate words and expressions.

widespread	health	wrong	environment
observe	recommendations	future	foresee

Zoologists study animals and how they live in their _____. They study classification, function, numbers, and overall _____ of various species of animals. Zoologists have to _____ and learn about habitats and threats in the field. Then, in the office, they write long reports and _____ on the conditions. It's not an easy job, but it is a very important one.

There have been many people throughout history who have predicted the _____. Looking back, some of them were _____ in their predictions. One renowned man said in the past that computers would not be so _____. But as we all know, they are a must these days. There's even a company named Future Savvy that tries to _____ what the future holds.

YOUTH TRADITIONS

Rites of Passage

Pre-reading Activity

Fill in the blanks using the following words: *New Zealand* and *Aborigines*

The indigenous people of Australia are also known as _____. While the first people to arrive on the much smaller islands of _____ are known as Maoris.

Preteens, teenagers, and young adults have historically had to perform a "rite   1
of passage" to demonstrate that they were passing from child to adult. The rites
of passage generally refer to some difficult tasks that youngsters would have to
perform successfully in order to be considered "adults" within their group.

Many know that Aboriginal boys in Australia were required to go on long   5
walks in the rough Australian outback for weeks at a time. They would have to do
this alone, survive the ordeal, and then return home. When the boy returned, the
tribe celebrated his new-found manhood.

Some Native American tribes require older children to go on a personal,
spiritual quest alone in the wilderness—uninhabited, mountainous areas. This   10
initiation ritual generally includes fasting and meditation. For a number of days,
they seek guidance to find the state where their spirits may be reborn within
them. Then they return and state their purpose in life and their role in the tribe.

The Orthodox Jewish faith requires boys and girls to study their religious
texts and memorize an enormous amount of them. The young must recite the   15
texts in front of a congregation of family and friends to show they are religiously
prepared for society. They are rewarded with a huge party called a Bar Mitzvah
for boys and Bat Mitzvah for girls. The celebration includes food and fabulous
gifts to mark their accomplishment and rite of passage.

Modern society has retained some of these ancient practices, but many   20
youth around the world no longer participate
in any event that demonstrates the passage
into adulthood. Is it necessary? As a preteen
or teen, would you like to do some <u>rigorous</u>
activity that proves that you are not a kid
anymore? In return, do you believe you
would be treated like an adult and have adult
responsibilities?

Reading Tips

The Outback is a vast, dry rural area of Australia. Less than 60,000 people inhabit the Outback along with a diverse set of animals such as kangaroos, wallabies, emus, and dingos. The term Outback is generally used to describe the emptiness, remoteness, and huge distances of inland Australia.

1   **What is the passage mainly about?**

a. the transition from youth to adulthood

b. new practices for youths in a modern society

c. the Aborigines who arrived in Australia long ago

d. the need for celebration for our children's growth

e. traditional rites of passage and their disappearance

2   **Which is closest in meaning to the word "rigorous"?**

a. punctual

b. religious

c. severe

d. vague

e. lax

3   **Which of the following is NOT true?**

a. Many of the traditional rites of passage are still performed.

b. American Indian boys go hungry during their spiritual quests.

c. Orthodox Jewish children recite religious texts for their rite of passage.

d. Most initiation rituals include rather challenging tasks for young children.

e. Aboriginal boys would go on walkabouts alone for weeks as a rite of passage.

4   **Which best fits in the blanks?**

> A rite of passage is a ritual event that marks a person's progress from one status to another — from _____ to adulthood. Each culture has its own rites of passage, but these days those events are _____.

a. childhood, growing up

b. adolescence, dying out

c. young adult, going on

d. traveler, showing up

e. wanderer, showing off

5   **What do Native American children do as an initiation rite?**

_____

The American Prom

Pre-reading Activity

1. Does your school have a dance at the end of the school year?
2. Does your school have a graduation at the end of the school year?
3. Have you been to a school dance or any kind of special dance occasion?

American teenagers have a tradition that marks the end of their high school experience and the beginning of their adult lives. This special event is called "prom." A prom is an evening that makes memories that can last a lifetime. Many elderly people can recall all the details of the night, even though it may have happened fifty years ago. It is truly a significant rite of passage.

The prom is usually a very formal occasion requiring the young men to wear tuxedos and the young women to wear formal gowns. Preparation for the prom begins weeks in advance with girls shopping for their dresses and boys securing their tuxedos at a rental store. On the day of the prom, the young ladies have their hair done in the latest fashion at a beauty salon, and a generous amount of time is spent applying make-up and polishing nails. The young gentlemen are busy with haircuts and picking up the corsage that their dates will wear on the wrist or fasten to the dress.

(1) Couples often hire limousines to take themselves to the prom destination. (2) Several couples will go to dinner together before or after the dance party. (3) The gym is decorated with giant rolls of colored paper adorned with stars or hearts to depict a romantic theme. (4) The <u>transformation</u> of the gym is complete with a welcoming archway or trellis laden with ribbons and flowers where couples will have their photographs taken sometime during the course of the evening. (5)

The prom is part of popular culture in the US, and it remains a tradition that has not changed so much in the last fifty-plus years. As an important step into adulthood, the prom is considered more significant since it provides a common bond from one generation to the next.

Reading Tips

clipped words

flu - influenza
gas - gasoline
vet - veterinarian
phone - telephone
prom - promenade
ad - advertisement
exam - examination
memo - memorandum
gym - gymnastics (or gymnasium)

1 **What is the passage mainly about?**

a. the American prom tradition as a rite of passage
b. the end of Americans' high school experience
c. the things American teenagers do at the prom
d. the clothes that are worn to a prom
e. the preparations for a prom night

2 **Which is closest in meaning to the word "transformation"?**

a. transportation
b. preservation
c. application
d. alteration
e. extent

3 **Which of the following is NOT true about the American prom?**

a. Young men dress up for the dance party.
b. Every American takes part in this rite of passage.
c. It is an important part of American high school culture.
d. It is an event that many senior citizens remember clearly.
e. Girls wear the corsage on prom night that their dates brought for them.

4 **Where does the following sentence best fit in the passage?**

> Sometimes a hotel is the site of the event, but more often it is held in the school gymnasium.

a. (1)   b. (2)   c. (3)   d. (4)   e. (5)

5 **What is the author's attitude toward the prom?**

a. sympathetic
b. indifferent
c. skeptical
d. negative
e. positive

A Words

A1. Fill in the blank according to the definition.

| quest | transformation | polish | adorn | wilderness |

1 _____: to decorate or add beauty to something
2 _____: to make something smooth and shiny by rubbing it
3 _____: a pursuit or journey made in order to find something
4 _____: a complete change or alteration in something or someone
5 _____: a large area of land that has never been cultivated or developed

A2. Choose the most appropriate word for each blank.

1 Brian, why don't you _____ your favorite poem for the class?
   a. recite   b. wear   c. customize   d. refresh

2 It's a casual occasion, so we are not required to dress up in _____ attire.
   a. formal   b. spiritual   c. economical   d. impolite

3 You'd better reserve the flight to Amsterdam in advance to _____ a seat.
   a. conquer   b. fasten   c. release   d. secure

4 Teams from colleges all over the country are here to _____ in the competition.
   a. belong   b. participate   c. argue   d. suspend

5 Many fraternities at North American universities have a(n) _____ for new members.
   a. balloon   b. archway   c. gymnasium   d. initiation

A3. Complete each sentence with one of the words from the box.

| congregation | generous | recall | meditation | generally |

1 It was astonishing to watch the band _____ at the concert.
2 It was _____ of you to donate money to relief organizations.
3 There is a church in Korea that has about 600,000 members in its _____.
4 Are you able to _____ the names of 20 of your elementary school friends?
5 The brainwaves of monks in _____ are similar to people who are sleeping.

B Expressions and Phrases

B1. Fill in the blank using an expression from the box.

at a time	in advance	even though	in return

1 If it is OK with you, I would like to pay for one month _____.
2 My best friend is always there for me without expecting anything _____.
3 People all around the world should try and reclaim the planet one inch _____.
4 _____ the boy knew he might get in trouble, he was not afraid of telling the truth.

B2. Complete each sentence with an expression from the reading passages.
   (Change the form of the verb if necessary.)

be rewarded with	prepare for	be busy with	refer to

1 Does anyone know what the number written in red _____?
2 My parents enrolled in the pension plan to _____ their retirement.
3 The 400-meter relay team _____ gold medals for their outstanding race.
4 The police department has _____ a string of robberies since last month.

C Summary

Complete the summary with the appropriate words and expressions.

formal	adulthood	modern	teenagers
transformed	performed	tuxedos	practices

Children and teenagers have historically _____ rites of passage to mark their entry into _____. From Aborigine boys in Australia to Orthodox Jewish children in many countries, these _____ have been around for a long time. While _____ society has largely lost many of these rites of passage, some cultures keep the tradition alive.

The prom is regarded as an important rite of passage for many American _____. This _____ occasion is planned far in advance—girls prepare their gowns, and boys get dressed up in _____. Even fancy limousines are hired, and the gym is _____ into a ballroom. The prom is a popular part of American culture and has remained so for decades.

BUTTERFLIES AND MOTHS

Butterfly Beauties

Pre-reading Activity

Fill in the blanks using the following words: *water*, *outside*, and *insects*

Butterflies and _____ have their skeletons on the _____ of their bodies, called the exoskeleton. This protects the insect and keeps _____ inside their bodies so they will not dry out.

Butterflies are interesting insects called *Lepidoptera*. Like all insects, butterflies have a head, thorax, abdomen, two antennae, and six legs. They are found on all continents except Antarctica, and it is estimated that there are approximately 12,000~15,000 species of butterflies in the world.

Butterflies have very colorful wings, but they do not get to enjoy the vast array of their own colors. This is because they can only see red, green, and yellow, and they are partially color-blind. Beautiful as they are, their beauty cannot last long. It is believed that butterflies have very short lifespans. An average butterfly species has an adult lifespan of two weeks or less. _____, one species found in Costa Rica has a life expectancy of about two days and lives ten days at the most. No adult butterfly can live more than a year.

Many butterflies migrate over long distances. They migrate for warmer temperatures and food. They feed primarily on nectar from flowers. Monarch butterflies are particularly famous for their migrations. Monarch butterflies in North America fly over 4,000~4,800 kilometers in the fall to get to warm areas and return north again in the spring.

There are more to butterflies than just their colorful beauty. Butterflies may look like <u>delicate</u>, gentle creatures, but they can carry 50 times their own body weight. <u>This</u> would be like an adult human lifting two heavy cars full of people. Butterflies are strong, fit, and amazing creatures, and they also play an important role as a pollinator. Despite their small size, butterflies are one of the world's most wondrous animals. Their beauty, seemingly miraculous metamorphosis, and carefree flight all spark our imaginations.

1
5
10
15
20

Reading Tips

types of butterflies

Grassland Butterflies : Monarchs, Crescentspot, Aphrodite, Viceroy

Woodland Butterflies : Acadian Hairstreak, Pine Butterfly, Comma Butterfly, Map Butterfly

Mountain Butterflies : Moorland Clouded Yellow, Piedmont Ringlet, Arctic Fritillary, Northern Blue, Creamy Marblewing

Exotic Butterflies of the Tropics : Paper Kite, Isabella, Blue Morpho

Endangered Species : Queen Alexandra's Birdwing, Zebra Swallowtail, Essex Emerald

1 **What is the passage mainly about?**

   a. the life expectancy of butterflies
   b. interesting facts about butterflies
   c. the colors that butterflies can see
   d. the Monarch butterfly of North America
   e. the miraculous transformation of butterflies

2 **Which is closest in meaning to the word "delicate"?**

   a. nasty
   b. graceful
   c. awkward
   d. miserable
   e. burdensome

3 **Which best fits in the blank?**

   a. However
   b. Furthermore
   c. For example
   d. In addition
   e. In fact

4 **Which of the following is true?**

   a. All of the adult butterflies live one day at the most.
   b. On average, butterflies can eat food using their two antennae.
   c. Owing to partial color-blindness, butterflies can only see black and white.
   d. Monarch butterflies fly south for warmer temperature in the fall.
   e. There are approximately 4,800 known species of butterflies around the world.

5 **What does the word "this" refer to?**

   _____

BUTTERFLIES AND MOTHS

The Deceptive Moth

Pre-reading Activity

True or False?

1. There are more than 150,000 species of moths throughout the world.	TRUE	FALSE
2. Moths can be differentiated from butterflies by the shape of their antennae.	TRUE	FALSE
3. Most moths are diurnal and are rarely seen at night.	TRUE	FALSE

The Cantonese speakers in Hong Kong have a name for it: the translation   1
is snake's head moth. The Italians call it the farfalla cobra. When you look at the
patterns on its wings, it is easy to see why there are people who put words like
snake, cobra, or some other serpent title in its name. For most of us, it is simply
known as the Atlas Moth—the biggest moth in the world. This is probably   5
because they have wingspans reaching 30 centimeters.

These large moths are found exclusively in tropical Southeast Asia, mostly
throughout the Malay Archipelago and parts of India. In Singapore, they are
abundant in the months of November and December. The Atlas moths are
commonly tawny to maroon in color with patterns on its wings that resemble a   10
snake's head. Maybe the purpose of the appearance is to play a role in predator
avoidance. Think about it, an attacking bird or any other predator would definitely
think twice before swooping down on the Atlas moth. The <u>deceptive</u> camouflage
even strikes fear in humans so that _____.

In India, like the Silkworm moth that belongs to a different but related   15
family, the Atlas moth cocoons also make silk strands. They are thought to be
more durable than those of the Silkworm moth. The Atlas moth cocoons are used
to produce purses and handbags in Taiwan.

As beautiful and cunning as the Atlas moth is, it does not get to enjoy a long
life. In fact, an adult Atlas moth lives for less than two weeks. Even if it wanted   20
to eat, it couldn't. It does not have a mouth. It simply lives off the reserves of fat
from when it was in the caterpillar
stage of its life. The job of the adult
Atlas moth is straightforward—the
males and females need to find each   25
other, mate, lay eggs, and die shortly
thereafter.

Reading Tips

be used to + verb
This machine is used to make glasses.

be/get used to + gerunds
David was used to working on difficult
assignments.
Chris hasn't got used to the new
system yet.

used to + verb
Jane used to enjoy gardening, but she
doesn't have time for it now.

1 **What is the passage mainly about?**

a. the names given to the Atlas moth

b. the habitat and diet of the Atlas moth

c. interesting facts about the Atlas moth

d. the size and appearance of the Atlas moth

e. the usefulness of the Atlas moth cocoons

2 **Which is closest in meaning to the word "deceptive"?**

a. misleading

b. interesting

c. controversial

d. pretentious

e. strange

3 **Which best fits in the blank?**

a. most people like their cunning nature

b. most people go to the zoo to watch them

c. many people like to raise them in their home

d. most people do not even want to touch them

e. most people enjoy watching them in the jungle

4 **Which of the following is NOT true?**

a. Predators cannot easily attack the Atlas moth.

b. The Atlas moth dies soon after the breeding season.

c. The Atlas moth's wing patterns are thought to confuse enemies.

d. The Atlas moth was given unique names due to its serpent-like patterns.

e. The silk of the Atlas moth cocoons is not as durable as that of the Silkworm.

5 **How do the adult Atlas moths manage to survive without mouths?**

_____

A Words

A1. Fill in the blank according to the definition.

caterpillar	migrate	reserve	continent	durable

1 _____: a large area of land such as Europe, Asia, and Africa

2 _____: lasting a long time in good condition without breaking

3 _____: a supply of something kept or stored for use when it is needed

4 _____: to move at a particular season from one part of the world to another

5 _____: a small, worm-like creature that develops into a butterfly or other flying insects

A2. Choose the most appropriate word for each blank.

1 It's easy for some people to be misled by _____ advertisements.
   a. deceptive   b. controversial   c. optimal   d. flexible

2 40 people died, and more than 2,000 were made homeless by the _____ storm.
   a. official   b. exclusive   c. tropical   d. ideal

3 The new military uniforms provide _____ when soldiers are in a forest.
   a. weapons   b. strength   c. camouflage   d. implement

4 The average _____ of some parts of the Arctic is below –60 degrees Celsius.
   a. temperature   b. lifespan   c. range   d. thermometer

5 She specializes in _____ from English to French and also the other way around.
   a. presentation   b. consent   c. migration   d. translation

A3. Complete each sentence with one of the words from the box.

predators	sparked	exclusively	serpent	abundant

1 Her latest single is sold _____ in our online store.

2 Most people seem to regard the _____ as cunning and subtle.

3 There is a(n) _____ supply of coffee coming out of South America.

4 Tigers and other big cats are _____, so they should not be owned as pets.

5 His racist comments in the interview _____ outrage throughout the country.

B

Expressions and Phrases

B1. Fill in the blank using an expression from the box.

at the most	even if	in fact	each other

1 The project is underway and should be finished within a year _____.
2 Though they are twin brothers, they have nothing in common with _____.
3 _____ you don't think you need any help at the moment, someday you will.
4 While it did not appear so, he was _____ eager to join the team and play soccer.

B2. Complete each sentence with an expression from the reading passages.
   (Change the form of the verb if necessary.)

live off	swoop down	belong to	feed on

1 The car that I drove yesterday actually _____ my little brother.
2 Hummingbirds _____ a variety of insects as well as the nectar of flowers.
3 The bald eagle _____ on a nesting gull and grabbed it up with its talons.
4 More and more people are retiring early and moving to the country to _____ the land.

C

Summary

Complete the summary with the appropriate words and expressions.

exclusively	wings	migrate	species
continent	weight	reserves	predators

Butterflies are small, delicate insects that are found on every _____ except Antarctica. Although there are thousands of _____, most of them live rather short lives—sometimes even just a couple of days long. However, butterflies are strong creatures in that they _____ long distances and carry 50 times their body _____.

The Atlas moth is considered the largest and most famous moth found _____ in tropical Southeast Asia. These large moths have _____ on the wings that look like a snake's head, and this definitely scares off _____. These moths don't have a mouth, so they survive entirely on fat _____ throughout their two-week adult life.

SAVING THE EARTH

The Enhanced Greenhouse Effect

Pre-reading Activity

Did you know?

The greenhouse effect is the natural process by which the atmosphere traps some of the Sun's energy. This effect helps warm the Earth enough to support living beings. However, due to the increase of greenhouse gases such as CO2, and methane, it is strengthened and may have serious consequences.

Perhaps the most long-lasting and potentially least reversible global problem today is the enhanced greenhouse effect. This effect is produced by too much carbon dioxide, methane, chlorofluorocarbons, and over a dozen other gases being pumped into the Earth's atmosphere. The role played by CO2 is the most significant. The amount of this gas in the atmosphere has risen steadily since the mid-1800s as a result of the combustion of coal, oil, and other fossil fuels on an ever-widening scale.

In the 1970s, the global CO2 level of the atmosphere was roughly 320 ppm, ___(A)___ the present atmospheric concentration of CO2 has increased to 380 ppm. If present trends in the emission of greenhouse gases, particularly CO2, continue to rise unchecked, climatic changes larger than any ever previously experienced may occur. This would substantially alter natural ecosystems, human and animal health, and the distribution of global resources. In addition, the enhanced greenhouse effect and subsequent global warming could continue to cause the rapid melting of polar ice, resulting in a rise in sea levels and the consequent flooding of coastal areas and cities. Global policy might then be formulated in order to find solutions to the various threats created from this phenomenon.

Another problem facing us with this dilemma is that many people are saying this phenomenon is a natural occurrence, and it is ___(B)___. Sadly, these people are relying on just a handful of scientists and <u>disregarding</u> the overwhelming majority of scientists who have clearly demonstrated the science behind this occurrence. Our science classrooms must do a better job in training current and future leaders who will help us turn this situation around.

1

5

10

15

20

25

Reading Tips

usage of "issue"

noun

1. a subject that people discuss; a social or political matter that affects the interests of many people
   Adoption is a highly controversial issue.

2. a magazine or newspaper that is published at a particular time
   Have you ever seen the latest issue of the Times?

1 **What is the second paragraph mainly about?**

a. our effort to cut down on fossil fuels

b. the phenomena caused by the increase of CO2

c. the way we can solve global warming in the future

d. the alternative energy we can use in the coming future

e. the reason why the CO2 level of the atmosphere has increased

2 **Which best fits in the blanks?**

	(A)		(B)
a.	as	···	exceptional
b.	though	···	natural
c.	if	···	unusual
d.	whereas	···	normal
e.	while	···	abnormal

3 **Which is closest in meaning to the word "disregarding"?**

a. ignoring

b. disgusting

c. depending

d. supporting

e. respecting

4 **What is the main cause for the enhanced greenhouse effect?**

a. lack of solutions to global warming

b. the melting of the polar ice and a rise in sea levels

c. ignorant people listening to a handful of scientists

d. the emission of carbon dioxide into our atmosphere

e. the altering of our natural ecosystems and our planet's health

5 **What can be inferred from the passage?**

a. Many companies will use alternative fuels.

b. We need a strong global policy for our environment.

c. The atmospheric concentration of CO2 can be unpredictable.

d. There is no correlation between global warming and the greenhouse effect.

e. The enhanced greenhouse effect is a natural phenomenon in the Earth's atmosphere.

SAVING THE EARTH

Environmental Solutions

Pre-reading Activity

Look at the title of the passage. Circle the words you think will be in the passage.

biological	energy resource	technology	clarify	preserve
useless	contributor	conglomerate	exhaustion	suppress

Now scan the passage, and see if you were right. How many? _____

The biggest contributor to the world's environmental problems has been our   1
choices for energy. We burn gas to fuel our cars. We burn coal to run our factories
and power electric plants. All the time, there are many other technologies that we
have known about for decades. These technologies will run our cars, heat our homes,
and provide our electricity. They are clean, or cleaner may be a more appropriate   5
word. These energy sources range from <u>harnessing</u> the power of the sun to the power
of the oceans' tides, to the numerous other emerging green technologies that people
are coming up with every day.

_____, these innovations and green technologies have been suppressed
by large oil companies, their lobbyists, and weak government leaders who cave in   10
to the multinational conglomerates. The big oil companies have known for quite
a while that once these new technologies become available, gas, coal, and other
pollution-creating fuels will go by the wayside.

While there has been some recent movement into green technologies, a lot of
families are tired of the slow pace and are going it alone. More and more families   15
are learning to build low-cost energy machines for their homes. They are learning
to build their own solar homes and are also putting small windmills and other
instruments in place to power their homes and sometimes their vehicles. These
pioneering families who are building their own free energy devices and machines are
leading the way into a brighter and cleaner future.   20

As these energy pioneers show how much money they save by using low-cost
energy machines, their neighbors will
want to do the same. We can expect
that this is how clean, low-cost
energy technologies will spread.
This is how green revolutions
will take place; by pioneering
individuals, not by governments
or large corporations.

Reading Tips

phrasal verbs "cave in"

1. to move or fall down from a roof or wall
   The roof of the house caved in on them.

2. to suddenly stop opposing something because someone has persuaded you
   He is expected to cave into the pressure to resign from public office.

1. **What is the main idea of the passage?**

   a. We have to use alternative fuel vehicles.

   b. We should find a way to invent alterative fuels.

   c. We can save the earth by using alternative fuels.

   d. More and more families are learning to build eco-houses.

   e. Government should cooperate with big companies to save energy.

2. **Which is closest in meaning to the word "harnessing"?**

   a. releasing

   b. consuming

   c. constraining

   d. expediting

   e. utilizing

3. **Which best fits in the blank?**

   a. Unfortunately

   b. Regardless

   c. Therefore

   d. Similarly

   e. Happily

4. **What is the author's attitude toward the energy pioneers?**

   a. neutral

   b. hopeful

   c. sarcastic

   d. sorrowful

   e. negative

5. **What will happen when green technologies become more possible?**

   _____

A Words

A1. Fill in the blank according to the definition.

substantially	conglomerate	pioneer	phenomenon	alter

1 _____: to make something or someone change
2 _____: by a large amount; in the most important way
3 _____: a situation or event that can be seen to happen
4 _____: a person who is the first to do something important
5 _____: a large business organization composed of several subsidiaries

A2. Choose the most appropriate word for each blank.

1 People can get hurt on the job if safety measures go _____ for too long.
   a. abundant   b. overwhelming   c. unchecked   d. steady

2 A lot of scientists are working to see if the aging process is somewhat _____.
   a. multinational   b. regarding   c. separate   d. reversible

3 The children _____ safety regulations, and that's why the accident happened.
   a. disregarded   b. respected   c. formulated   d. demonstrated

4 They state that the report has been intentionally _____ by the authorities.
   a. emerged   b. suppressed   c. contaminated   d. tolerated

5 The concentration of gas-guzzling vehicles in our big cities leads to _____ problems.
   a. environmental   b. physical   c. cognitive   d. available

A3. Complete each sentence with one of the words from the box.

environmental	dilemma	solar	contributor	harness

1 Al Gore is a major _____ to raising environmental awareness.
2 The biggest _____ facing South Africa is racial discrimination.
3 Recently there have been many _____ in the ways people communicate.
4 To generate electricity, we can _____ solar energy in massive amounts.
5 Before long, we may have vehicles that are not only electric but also _____.

B Expressions and Phrases

B1. Fill in the blank using an expression from the box.

as a result of	in addition	a handful of	all the time

1 _____ obesity, the number of heart-related deaths has doubled.
2 Only _____ people came to the public meeting, so it was canceled.
3 I think there is something wrong with me, because I am hungry _____.
4 Due to the computer crash, many finance documents were lost. _____, we lost important contracts.

B2. Complete each sentence with an expression from the reading passages. (Change the form of the verb if necessary.)

take place	rely on	go by the wayside	be tired of

1 Sometimes we need to _____ our instinct without trusting anyone.
2 The kids said that they _____ having eggs and toast for breakfast.
3 I think traditional television will _____ because of HD and the Internet.
4 Have you heard about the summer music festival that will _____ next week?

C Summary

Complete the summary with the appropriate words and expressions.

alternative	long-lasting	pumped	suppressing
pioneers	phenomenon	human	environment

The enhanced greenhouse effect is the most _____ global problem. It was mainly caused by too much CO2 being _____ into the Earth's atmosphere. If this trend continues, our environment will change a lot. Many consider this a naturally occurring _____ and not the result of _____ action.

Our energy choices are hurting the _____. While new alternative technologies have existed for a long time, big oil companies are _____ them. This is continuing to slow down the innovation and use of _____ sources of energy. Many energy _____ are trying to lead a green revolution from the ground up.

TECHNOLOGY

CIA Gadgets—Past and Present

Pre-reading Activity

True or false?

1. CIA stands for Central Intelligence Association.	TRUE	FALSE
2. One of the CIA's jobs is to collect information about foreign governments.	TRUE	FALSE
3. Most specialists working at the CIA are from the army.	TRUE	FALSE

You have probably heard people talk about the "CIA" in movies, books, and   1
newspapers. You may even know it stands for Central Intelligence Agency. The
CIA is the American governmental agency made famous by Hollywood because
of its spies and their dangerous lifestyles. One of the aspects of their lives that
many people are attracted to is the tools and gadgets that the spies use.   5

The CIA has opened a museum for the public to view gadgets not used
by agents anymore. There are many <u>ingenious</u> gadgets in the museum that
demonstrate the creativity of the inventors. The listening devices that the CIA had
in Asian jungles during the Vietnam War were shaped like animal dung. Nobody
would pick up animal feces so they were never noticed by the soldiers being   10
spied on. Another jungle listening device was the remote-controlled dragonfly.
When spies wanted to listen in, they would just send in the dragonflies by remote
control. The dragonflies would fly around in the air and _____.
If the CIA needed photos, they had miniature cameras that they could strap on to
the chests of pigeons. Some of these cameras were a failure in that the cameras   15
were too heavy for the pigeons, and <u>they</u> ended up just
walking instead of flying overhead to take photos.

Some of the more recent technologies are interesting
as well. They have special dust they spread on the
ground in the areas of war or conflict. The dust picks   20
up the enemy movement and tells the CIA where they
are and where they are going. If the CIA gets your
pictures? Well, watch out, or they will find you.
They can plug a photo into the Internet, and the
software will scan the entire web and even home
computers for people with the identical noses,
chins, or other parts. It's pretty neat stuff, isn't it?

Reading Tips

The CIA (Central Intelligence
Agency) is the department of
the US government that collects
secret political, military, and other
information about other countries
and protects secret information
about the U.S.A. The CIA also
engages in covert activities at the
request of the President of the
U.S.A.

1   **What is the passage mainly about?**

a. the neat spy gear used by the CIA

b. the CIA's important task—the spies

c. the CIA as the US governmental agency

d. the brilliant spies who worked for the CIA

e. the museum exhibiting up-to-date spy devices

2   **Which is closest in meaning to the word "ingenious"?**

a. trivial

b. clumsy

c. brilliant

d. incompetent

e. commonplace

3   **Which best fits in the blank?**

a. look for their mates

b. capture the enemy alive

c. record the conversations

d. call a truce with the enemy

e. distract the soldiers with a noise

4   **What does the word "they" refer to?**

a. photos

b. the CIA

c. the pigeons

d. the cameras

e. the chests of pigeons

5   **What can be inferred from the passage?**

a. The museum houses very old-fashioned spy tools.

b. Some of the modern spy gadgets are available on the market.

c. Overhearing conversations is against the law during warfare.

d. The CIA may use facial recognition software to catch bad guys.

e. The CIA gadgets are mainly used to obtain personal information.

TECHNOLOGY

The Copenhagen Wheel

02

Pre-reading Activity

What do you think is the best way to reduce air pollution?

_____

Do you think we can reduce pollution by using public transportation?

_____

Can you imagine a bicycle that has an iPhone on its handlebar and provides 1
navigation tools and fitness information, along with data collectors that measure
air pollution? This is just the beginning of the list of things that this dynamic new
bicycle, known as the Copenhagen Wheel, is capable of. The most distinctive
feature of this bike is its red hub on the rear wheel, where the brain of the bike 5
stores power, boosts speed, monitors the rider's exercise, and collects data from
the air and the environment. The data that is collected is put onto a public website
so city residents can find out what their urban atmosphere is like during the day.

The Copenhagen Wheel comes to us from the Massachusetts Institute
of Technology in the U.S.A. It was developed by a part of MIT that is putting 10
"intelligence" into everyday items that are a part of the infrastructure of our
cities. Researchers from MIT chose the Copenhagen Conference on Climate
Change to <u>show off</u> the new bicycle wheel, and early feedback was very positive.

In its simplest definition, the goal of the Copenhagen Wheel project is to
promote cycling by extending the distance people can cover. In addition, the 15
makers ensure the whole bike riding experience is smoother so that even steep
inclines are no longer a barrier to comfortable cycling. This new bicycle is also
perfect for protecting the environment by reducing emissions, and many big
cities are making plans to encourage their residents to use this innovative two-
wheeler when they commute to and from work. The director of the Copenhagen 20
Wheel project, Christine Outram, expects that this new bike will help lead the
charge of smart transportation into the 21st
century. She is fully convinced that many major
metropolitan cities will see the benefits of
promoting this type of cycling to their 25
residents.

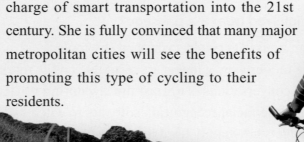

Reading Tips

phrasal verbs with "put"

put away : to put something in
the place where you usually keep
it when you are not using it
She put the notebook away and stood
up.

put down : to put someone or
something onto a surface
Ann put her raincoat down and went
upstairs.

put out : to make something stop
burning
It took firefighters five hours to put the
blaze out.

put off : to delay doing
something
I couldn't put the decision off any
longer.

1   What is the passage mainly about?

   a. a new wheel that will be put on bicycles
   b. a team at MIT that invented a new bicycle
   c. a practical way to promote the use of bicycles
   d. an eco-friendly bicycle with cutting-edge features
   e. how the innovative bike will replace cars in big cities

2   Which is the closest in meaning to the phrase "show off"?

   a. purchase
   b. regulate
   c. organize
   d. assemble
   e. demonstrate

3   What can be inferred from the passage?

   a. If more people ride bicycles, more people will also take their cars.
   b. If more people ride bicycles, there will be less traffic on the roads.
   c. If more people ride bicycles, the environment pollution will get worse.
   d. If more people ride bicycles, there will be more arguments on the streets.
   e. If more people ride bicycles, the residents will often use the subway.

4   Which best fits in the blanks?

   The ingenious bike called the Copenhagen Wheel was _____ by MIT. It
   will promote cycling by _____ the range people can bike and ultimately
   benefit our environment.

   a. created, decreasing   b. made, fitting   c. shown, cutting
   d. invented, increasing   e. changed, considering

5   What are the purposes of the Copenhagen Wheel project?

   _____

A Words

A1. Fill in the blank according to the definition.

conflict	gadget	emission	distinctive	promote

1 _____: a small tool that does something useful

2 _____: a gas or other substance that goes into the air

3 _____: to help or encourage something to develop; to advance in rank

4 _____: having a characteristic which makes something recognized easily

5 _____: a prolonged struggle; a state of argument between people or groups

A2. Choose the most appropriate word for each blank.

1 The time that is taken to _____ from Osaka to Kyoto is not worth it.
  a. commute   b. commit   c. commune   d. communicate

2 Doctors feel we need to get more exposure to sunlight to _____ our Vitamin D.
  a. boost   b. plug   c. rear   d. range

3 The new electric vehicle can _____ over 400 kilometers on one battery charge.
  a. demonstrate   b. cover   c. extend   d. expand

4 Tom and Donald are _____ twins, so that I cannot tell them apart unless they speak.
  a. fraternal   b. Siamese   c. sophomore   d. identical

5 Although she searched the _____ neighborhood for her puppy, it was nowhere to be found.
  a. dynamic   b. incomplete   c. neat   d. entire

A3. Complete each sentence with one of the words from the box.

infrastructure	innovative	navigation	metropolitan	incline

1 On the treadmill, I use a 12% _____ in order to get a better workout.

2 There are many _____ cities popping up in China on a yearly basis.

3 This new cell phone is described as the most _____ product of the year.

4 The GPS _____ system went out, and the sailors had to use the stars.

5 The Chinese are investing billions of dollars into the _____ of their country.

B Expressions and Phrases

B1. Fill in the blank using an expression from the box.

in that	along with	no longer	as well

1 Whenever Judy is driving, she sings _____ the radio.
2 The DSLR is much better _____ it produces better picture quality.
3 Kate is fluent in Spanish, and she speaks Russian a little bit _____.
4 Pluto, unfortunately, is _____ counted as our solar system's ninth planet.

B2. Complete each sentence with an expression from the reading passages.
(Change the form of the verb if necessary.)

listen in	watch out	end up	stand for

1 Yesterday I fell asleep on the subway and _____ at the last station.
2 If a truck is coming down the road too fast, you had better _____!
3 She _____ on her parents and heard they were going to get her a new car.
4 By now, most of us know that NBA _____ the National Basketball Association.

C Summary

Complete the summary with the appropriate words and expressions.

researchers	governmental	navigate	gadgets
delicate	promote	lifestyles	transportation

The CIA, the American _____ agency, is popular in Hollywood due to its spies and their dangerous _____. This agency is famous for its ingenious spy _____. You can see many cool things that are no longer used at a museum. Naturally, the spy gear used by the CIA is very _____.

The Copenhagen Wheel is a dynamic new bicycle that can help you _____ city streets, store weather information, and much more. This bicycle comes to us from the _____ at MIT. The aim of the Copenhagen Wheel project is to _____ cycling and protect our environment. It will lead the charge of smart _____ in the 21st century.

POLITICAL SCIENCE IN ACTION

The Berlin Wall and Its Legacy

Pre-reading Activity

Did you know?
World War II (1939-45) was a war involving almost every major country in the world. One side was the Allies (the UK, France, Poland, the U.S.A., and the Soviet Union), and the other side was the Axis (Germany, Japan, and Italy). The war was started by Adolf Hitler who intended to increase German power by attacking other countries. The war ended when Germany was defeated.

The Berlin Wall, dividing the German capital, came to symbolize the Cold War tensions between the world's two superpowers—the US and the Soviet Union—that escalated after World War II. East Germany would become a communist state, while West Germany would be a capitalist, US-backed government in control of daily affairs. 1

It is now known that the Soviet leader, Joseph Stalin, had plans to include all of Germany as one of the Communist satellites, but that would never come to be as the U.S.A. and other Allied countries stayed in the region. Although Berlin was located in East Germany, the city was divided between the Allied victors of the war. The sectors of the Western Allies—the United States, the United Kingdom, and France—formed West Berlin, while the Soviet sector formed East Berlin. For a couple of decades after the war, passage between the two separated Berlins, though severely <u>restricted</u>, was more relaxed than it would eventually become. Berlin was viewed as the best place to cross over to the more open West Germany, especially for ambitious young Germans. 5 10

The East Germans and their Soviet backers knew the country was losing a lot of people, and this was becoming an embarrassment. So, in 1961, construction of the Berlin Wall began. First, the city was divided by barbed wire fences and then by stronger fortifications. Afterwards, many families were separated, and West Berlin became an island in Communist East Germany. 15

The wall was a physical symbol of the figurative Iron Curtain dividing Communism from Capitalism. Only when Mikhail Gorbachev became the head of the Union of Soviet Socialist Republics, was there a thawing of relations. Gorbachev visited the United States, befriended world leaders, and reformed the economies of the Eastern bloc. Finally, in 1989, it was announced that _____, and people from East Berlin climbed over to the other side to celebrate the coming union. 20

Reading Tips

usage of "passage"

1. a portion or section of a book, speech, or piece of music
   Read the passage from chapter 2.

2. a long narrow space with walls on both sides which connects one place to another
   There is an underground passage leading from the castle to the outside.

3. a progress from one situation or one stage in development to another
   The passage from kindergarten to elementary school is an important transition.

1   What is the passage mainly about?

   a. the Cold War between the superpowers
   b. the beginning and end of the Berlin Wall
   c. Gorbachev's contributions to the end of the Cold War
   d. the sharp conflict between Communism and Capitalism
   e. how the Berlin Wall divided Germany into two countries

2   Which is closest in meaning to the word "restricted"?

   a. released
   b. convicted
   c. restrained
   d. overcome
   e. proclaimed

3   Which best fits in the blank?

   a. the wall would be completely torn down
   b. the wall would be rebuilt as soon as possible
   c. the wall would be temporarily opened during the day
   d. anyone could pass through the wall if he/she had a visa
   e. the access to West Berlin from East Germany would be easy

4   Which of the following is NOT true?

   a. The Berlin Wall was built by East Germans and their Soviet backers.
   b. A lot of West Germans moved to East Germany with great ambition.
   c. After World War II, Germany was divided into two separate countries.
   d. West Berlin, which became capitalist, remained isolated by the Berlin Wall.
   e. The victors of World War II were the U.S.A., the UK, France, and the Soviet Union.

5   What is the type of the passage?

   a. nostalgic
   b. persuasive
   c. informative
   d. comparative
   e. argumentative

Tiananmen Square

Pre-reading Activity

Circle the countries which are communist.
[Hint: There are five communist countries.]

China	North Korea	Vietnam	Canada	Laos
France	Cuba	Switzerland	Spain	New Zealand

Deng Xiaoping was the chairman of the Chinese Communist Party after 1
the death of Mao Zedong. After the brutal repression of Mao, Deng Xiaoping's
economically-liberal policies created an atmosphere of hope. With the Eastern
Communist bloc's downfall, many Chinese began to expect the same reforms in
China, namely democratization and a more free capitalist society. 5

Deng Xiaoping sought a compromise between traditional Marxism and the
pressure of modernization. He placed some large cities as special economic zones
where free-market capitalism could take place. He intended to see how Chinese-
styled capitalism would work in these zones, and the policy in general <u>reaped</u> positive
results. This led to the gradual implementation of a market economy and some political 10
liberation that relaxed the system organized by Mao.

_____, some students and intellectuals thought that the reforms were not
enough to meet their desire for democratization and that China needed to change its
political system. They believed Chinese reforms should mirror the reforms Gorbachev
was making in the Soviet Union. Even Hu Yaobang, the General Secretary of the 15
Communist Party of China, voiced calls for economic change and democratic reform
within the structure of the government. But he was eventually chastised, driven out of
office, and died soon thereafter.

Many Chinese thought democracy and free speech would accompany the
economic reform, so Hu's death caused nationwide demonstrations. Protestors gathered 20
at Tiananman Square to express their displeasure with the Chinese Communist Party,
expecting that the pressure of the public would move the party leaders. Instead,
tanks were ordered to fire on the crowds, and many arrests were made. The protest
lasted seven weeks, and a great number of people were killed. This event would be
remembered as the crushing of the hopes of democracy. 25

Reading Tips

suffix "-wide"

extending or applying throughout
the given place or area

citywide
worldwide
countrywide
nationwide

1   **What is the passage mainly about?**

    a. the protesters' full support of Deng Xiaoping's reform
    b. the CCP's crackdown on protesters in Tiananmen Square
    c. long-cherished hope for democracy and economic reform
    d. a great outpouring of mourning for Hu Yaobang's sudden death
    e. the background and historical significance of Tiananmen Square protests

2   **Which is closest in meaning to the word "reaped"?**

    a. advocated
    b. abandoned
    c. reproduced
    d. discouraged
    e. accomplished

3   **Which best fits in the blank?**

    a. However
    b. Therefore
    c. In other words
    d. For instance
    e. Furthermore

4   **Which of following is true?**

    a. Deng Xiaoping was strongly influenced by Gorbachev's thought.
    b. The protests were mostly sparked by the death of Mao Zedong.
    c. Change was not going to come as quickly as the protestors had hoped.
    d. Freedom of speech was guaranteed during the time of Deng Xiaoping.
    e. The Tianman Square massacre brought a change in the political system of the CCP.

5   **Which best fits in the blanks?**

> Many Chinese hoped that China would be a _____ country, but their expectation was not met. As a result, a protest for political and economic reform was held at Tiananmen Square, and the CCP _____ on the protesters.

    a. communist, looked down   b. neutral, pulled down
    c. democratic, cracked down   d. liberal, paid down
    e. bureaucratic, brought down

A Words

A1. Fill in the blank according to the definition.

satellite	fortification	superpower	chastise	liberation

1 _____: to criticize someone severely
2 _____: a city or country that is controlled by a larger one
3 _____: the process of making walls or buildings stronger to defend
4 _____: a country that has very great military, economic, and political power
5 _____: the act of freeing someone from feelings or conditions that make their life unhappy

A2. Choose the most appropriate word for each blank.

1 Ron was intensely _____, obsessed with the idea of becoming famous.
   a. content   b. embarrassing   c. awkward   d. ambitious

2 They're still trying to find _____ for the ship canal development scheme.
   a. victors   b. liberators   c. backers   d. beginners

3 The _____ truth is that many children in Africa starve to death every day.
   a. sophisticated   b. brutal   c. energy   d. figurative

4 The demonstrators at the G20 summit in Canada _____ their displeasure.
   a. voiced   b. sparked   c. prescribed   d. restricted

5 Yesterday at the national convention, there was a(n) _____ against the company.
   a. suggestion   b. instruction   c. organization   d. demonstration

A3. Complete each sentence with one of the words from the box.

befriended	symbol	nationwide	compromise	severely

1 At last, the government and the labor union managed to reach a _____.
2 In England, a _____ search is underway to find a missing French tourist.
3 Tony _____ me when I first arrived in New York as an exchange student.
4 The Statue of Liberty standing in New York harbor is a _____ of freedom.
5 Relations between the two countries have been _____ damaged by the incident.

B Expressions and Phrases

B1. Fill in the blank using an expression from the box.

in general	a couple of	in control of	afterwards

1 I need _____ books to read during the long flight to Paris.
2 Jackson is the person _____ all the decision-making on the project.
3 Let's go and see *Shrek Forever After* and go out for a meal _____.
4 _____, my opinion is that politicians who break the law should be punished.

B2. Complete each sentence with an expression from the reading passages.
(Change the form of the verb if necessary.)

cross over	tear down	be driven out of	take place

1 Senator Lilly _____ politics after the scandal became public.
2 A Russian spy named Philip wants to _____ to the United States.
3 Those old houses should have been _____ to make way for the new road.
4 The fireworks' display will _____ on the riverside in the last week of July.

C Summary

Complete the summary with the appropriate words and expressions.

ambitious	constructed	capitalism	cracked down
symbol	divided	reformed	economic

The Berlin Wall was a(n) _____ of the Cold War. While Berlin was in East Germany, the city was _____ among four countries including the U.S.A. and the Soviet Union. Many _____ people tried to flee to West Berlin, and the Berlin Wall was _____ to stop this flow. In 1989, it was finally torn down.

Deng Xiaoping, the leader of the Chinese Communist Party, _____ some economic policies after Mao Zedong. But it didn't satisfy young Chinese hoping for democratization and _____. Provoked by the death of Hu Yaobang who voiced calls for _____ and political reform, many protesters demonstrated at Tiananmen Square, and the CCP _____ hard on the protesters.

LIVING CREATURES

Does the Earth Breathe?

Pre-reading Activity

Fill in the blanks using the following words: *interacts*, *exist*, and *species*

The Earth is a home to millions of _____ including humans and is currently the only place in the universe where life is known to _____. The planet formed 4.54 billion years ago. The Earth _____ with other objects in space, especially the Sun and the Moon.

Astrophysicists in Russia have been studying to see if the Earth actually breathes just like all living creatures. Somewhat surprisingly to some people, they have determined that the Earth does in fact breathe. They summarized their findings by saying the Earth is a living thing or organism just like humans, trees, plants, bacteria, and all other types of life that the Earth supports. Some of these scientists are going one step further by saying the Earth even appears to have feelings.

Whereas we breathe air, the Earth appears to breathe energy. The Russian scientists measured the daily energy that our Earth inhales and exhales through powerful monitors, telescopes, and other scientific instruments. They found that different parts of the Earth breathe a bit differently. Like humans, the Earth breathes slowly and quietly at night. As dawn breaks, (1) it begins to breathe heavier starting with its first morning breath. It seems that the Earth wakes up just like people do. Scientists can tell what time (2) it wakes up by its sudden rapid "breathing" rate. In this way, scientists can tell when it goes to sleep as well.

What is interesting is how much the Earth _____. The scientists found that when wars are going on, the earth breathes really rapidly as if (3) it is "worried" or "upset." However, when many people around the world celebrate holidays or when people tend to be more relaxed, the Earth is also more relaxed. According to the Russian scientists, the most important lesson that they want humans to learn from this is that the Earth feels us. (4) It feels our happiness, our peacefulness, and even our fears. Based on this research, (5) it appears the Earth does not like us to fight. It likes us to be happy and peaceful. Whether you believe the Russian scientists or not, the hypothesis does seem to make a lot of sense.

Reading Tips

usage of "whereas"

conjunction

used to compare two people, things, situations and describe that there is an important difference between them

The old computer system was quite complicated whereas the new system is really very simple.

Whereas knowledge can be acquired from books, skills must be learned through practice.

1 **What is the passage mainly about?**

a. the Russian scientific community and some of their hypotheses

b. reasons that the Earth feels happy and sometimes worried or upset

c. the scientific instruments for measuring the amount of the Earth's breathing

d. an assumption that the Earth breathes and feels just like other living creatures

e. detailed explanations for why the Earth sometimes gets mad at human beings

2 **Which best fits in the blank?**

a. rotates on its axis

b. is affected by energy

c. reacts to human events

d. embraces human beings

e. changes its appearance

3 **Which is closest in meaning to the word "hypothesis"?**

a. proof

b. doubt

c. suggestion

d. affirmation

e. memorandum

4 **Choose the underlined "it" which refers to a different noun.**

a. (1)   b. (2)   c. (3)   d. (4)   e. (5)

5 **What can be inferred from this passage?**

a. The Earth's feelings may have a big effect on human beings.

b. The activity of the earth can be changed by human action.

c. Each and every part of the Earth interacts with human beings.

d. Humans are more intelligent than other living organisms on Earth.

e. The Earth reacts violently to people who wage wars against nations.

What Do Plants Like?

Pre-reading Activity

Did you know?
1. There are about 350,000 species of plants on the earth.
2. Plants are defined as seed plants, bryophytes, ferns, and fern allies.
3. Much of human nutrition depends on land plants, either directly or indirectly.

Lots of students do experiments on plants for their science projects. Scientists do this as well. Have you ever heard of a lie detector machine? It is something that police can hook up to people to figure out if they are lying or not. The machine can feel the energy in your body. If your energy moves fast, it shows you are nervous and may be lying. If it is slow and steady, it shows you are relaxed and probably not being deceitful.

Scientists have attached these same machines to plants, not to see if they are lying of course. They put the machines onto plants to see what makes them nervous, what makes them calm, and what makes them excited. They found many interesting things. First, they discovered when live fish were being cut for sushi or live lobsters were being boiled, the plants got very upset. They seemed to respond to the fear of the live sea creatures.

(1) Equally as interesting, they found the plants actually got excited when their owners were coming home. (2) What is even more <u>intriguing</u> is the plants got excited at the moment when the owner left his/her office to come home. (3) It seems that the plants get so connected with their owner that they could pick up their owner's intention to come home.

(4) When the owner pulled out the scissors to trim the plants, the plants got upset. Scientists tried to trick the plants and pretend they were going to cut them. The plants did not get nervous in that case. (5) It was as if they could read the owner's mind. They knew they would not be cut. So, when taking care of your plants, remember that they are sensitive, smart, and quite possibly psychic.

Reading Tips

"lie" & "lay"

lie
1. to be in a position in which your body is on a surface (lie – lay – lain)
   He is lying on the bed watching TV.
2. to say something that is not true (lie – lied – lied)
   It was obvious that Jason was lying.

lay (lay – laid – laid)
to put someone or something down in a careful way, especially so that it is lying flat
She laid her hand on my head.

1   What is the passage mainly about?

   a. a lie detector that notices the feelings of plants

   b. some studies that highlight the intelligence of plants

   c. some findings that show plants interact with other creatures

   d. plants that strongly influence changes of the owners' mind

   e. some experiments that demonstrate the consciousness of plants

2   Which is closest in meaning to the word "intriguing"?

   a. curious

   b. tedious

   c. reliable

   d. exclusive

   e. disgusting

3   Where does the following sentence best fit in the passage?

> Plants also seemed not to like to be cut.

   a. (1)   b. (2)   c. (3)   d. (4)   e. (5)

4   What can be inferred from the passage?

   a. Plants may fight back when they are threatened.

   b. Plants possibly get more relaxed when they are alone.

   c. Plants may start to droop when they are in a bad mood.

   d. Plants like a place where they can get fresh air and sunshine.

   e. Plants probably know when they are not cared for by their owners.

5   Why did scientists connect lie detector machines to plants?

_____

Unit Review

A Words

A1. Fill in the blank according to the definition.

> inhale   hypothesis   deceitful   telescope   intention

1 _____: acting dishonestly in order to trick people
2 _____: an act of determining to take some action
3 _____: to breathe air, smoke, or other substance into your lungs
4 _____: a piece of equipment used for making distant objects look closer and larger
5 _____: an idea that attempts to explain something that has not yet been proven to be true

A2. Choose the most appropriate word for each blank.

1 He is a(n) _____ that works at the Rose Center for Earth and Space.
   a. astrophysicist   b. astrologer   c. advertiser   d. photographer

2 Many heard a(n) _____ succession of gunshots in the heart of the city.
   a. intriguing   b. rapid   c. determined   d. fun

3 A mistake made during the _____ led to the discovery of other uses.
   a. detection   b. experiment   c. examination   d. conference

4 The authorities are trying to avoid answering questions about _____ issues.
   a. peaceful   b. steady   c. sensitive   d. scientific

5 As you know, the most common expression on Halloween is "_____ or Treat."
   a. Trap   b. Trike   c. Train   d. Trick

A3. Complete each sentence with one of the words from the box.

> breathe   energy   boiling   scissors   nervous

1 My little brother cut me with _____ by mistake.
2 Walking through a dark, dense forest really makes me _____.
3 I didn't even have the _____ to get out of bed, so I couldn't go to work.
4 If you know a seizure is oncoming, you need to sit down and _____ deeply.
5 After _____ the noodles for 4 minutes, immediately rinse them with cold water.

B Expressions and Phrases

B1. Fill in the blank using an expression from the box.

as if	just like	according to	at the moment

1 Mr. Smith is busy _____. Can I take a message?

2 _____ a recent poll, there is now widespread criticism of the bill.

3 I think that pets should be given love and attention _____ people.

4 When I arrived in Paris, it looked _____ it had been raining. The streets were still wet.

B2. Complete each sentence with an expression from the reading passages.
   (Change the form of the verb if necessary.)

go on	make sense	pull out	take care of

1 He reached into the bag and _____ my birthday present.

2 It doesn't _____ that Ron did such a foolish thing. He is a good student.

3 She _____ the elderly so well that she wants to work in a senior citizen home.

4 While World War II was _____, many Jews had to flee Europe and find new homes.

C Summary

Complete the summary with the appropriate words and expressions.

trim	determined	carefully	experiments
feelings	excited	changes	hypothesis

Russian astrophysicists have _____ that the Earth breathes like other living creatures. In addition, they believe the Earth even appears to have _____. They found that the activity of the Earth _____ according to human action. The Earth tends to be worried when things are bad, and happy when things are good. Do you believe this _____?

Scientists are doing some unusual _____. They have hooked up plants to a lie detector to see if they can pick up energy from plants. The results of the experiments are surprising. Some plants got "_____" when their owners came home. Others got upset when the owners were going to give them a(n) _____. Like this, plants have their own emotion, so we had better look after them more _____.

FAMILY

The Changing Family

Pre-reading Activity

Agree or Disagree?

1. Children from a poor country should be adopted to a rich country.	AGREE DISAGREE
2. Single people should be allowed to adopt a child.	AGREE DISAGREE
3. Adopted children should be given a chance to meet their biological parents.	AGREE DISAGREE

A family means a group of people who are related to each other by blood or marriage and share a close relationship with one another. It usually consists of a married couple and their children.

Throughout human history, members of the family have changed, and the definition of the family is also changing all around the world. Western countries are taking the lead in redefining the family unit. Because countries like the U.S.A. dominate the global media, it is expected that western family trends will spread around the world. Let's look at these new trends. Primarily, we are seeing that westerners are becoming more interested in adoption. Many famous celebrities are adopting children, and this goes a long way in changing the status quo. One of the world's most glamorous power couples—Angelina Jolie and Brad Pitt—are not even married but have adopted children from orphanages around the world.

Many single female stars such as the singer Madonna are also adopting children from African orphanages. Madonna has gone into the poorest countries in the world such as Malawi and has adopted children and supported the orphanages there. Previous to Madonna, non-Africans were not even allowed to adopt children from Malawi.

As recently as a decade ago, US law and orphanages around the world did not want to allow single parents, unmarried couples, or friends to adopt children, but because of the large numbers of orphans, they have altered the rules. This is a great trend to celebrate and encourage. What a noble, wonderful thing to do! Providing a child with a loving, safe home is such a wonderful gift to the world.

1

5

10

15

20

25

Reading Tips

Latin words and phrases used in English

per: for each
id est(i.e.): that is
bona fide: genuine
versus(vs.): against
et cetera(etc.): and so on
exempli gratia(e.g.): for example
vice versa: the other way round
status quo: existing state of affairs
ad hoc: formed or done for a
　　　particular purpose only

1   **What is the passage mainly about?**

a. the legal process of adopting a child
b. learning the importance of the family
c. holding to traditional family structures
d. describing forms of celebrities' adoption
e. the change of the public perception regarding a family unit

2   **Which is closest in meaning to the word "trend"?**

a. emergency
b. inference
c. tendency
d. tolerance
e. energy

3   **What is the author's attitude toward adoption?**

a. Adoption should be very tightly regulated.
b. Adoption should be a married couple's first option.
c. Only qualified married couples should adopt a child.
d. People who want to adopt should be allowed to do so.
e. Celebrities and other famous people should not adopt children.

4   **What can be inferred from the passage?**

a. The process of adoption has become more complicated than before.
b. Celebrity' adoptions provide a model that other people follow.
c. Africans will easily be allowed to adopt a child in the future.
d. The number of orphans worldwide is steadily increasing.
e. It is impossible for an unmarried couple to adopt a child.

5   **What does the word "this" refer to?**

_____

The Changing Face of Marriage

Pre-reading Activity

Did you know?
1. Each year 2.3 million couples wed, and 1 million couples divorce in the U.S.A.
2. The average age of a bride is 25.3, and the average age of a groom is 26.9.
3. 80 percent of weddings are performed in churches in the U.S.A.

Marriage is a social or legal contract between a male and a female who love each other. But marriage based on romantic love is a relatively recent idea. According to different cultures and customs, marriage age and the reasons for marriage have varied greatly. For example, in ancient Rome, many young girls married in their early teens. In the Middle Ages, romantic love was not considered essential in a marriage. It was more or less a business contract.

Over the last couple of hundred years, the definition of marriage and the average marriage age have changed a lot. Today, marriage is a big part of our life and is regarded as a symbol of love, not business. In some countries, the average marriage age is rising. Many sociologists feel this is due to the fact that people prefer to marry after they complete their education and have stable employment. Career aspirations have also begun to <u>outweigh</u> the importance of marriage.

More and more women want to achieve educational levels equal to those of men and enter the job market at the same level. Many women regard marriage as something to be delayed until "the right time." These are factors which may be considered when discussing appropriate age or conditions for marriage.

Some sociologists expect more changes in "marriage" and "family organization" in the future. Because of societal trends like extended lifespan, some think tanks predict either people will marry numerous times or some societies may do away with marriage entirely. Words like co-parenting, where arrangements are put in place to raise children outside of marriage, will come into our vocabulary. Be prepared for many changes in the family structure in your lifetime.

1
5
10
15
20
25

Reading Tips

prefix "out-"

outlive : to remain alive after someone else has died
She outlived her sister.

outgrow: to grow too big for something
Jason outgrows his clothes so quickly.

outrun: to run faster than someone else
Do you think a woman can outrun a man?

1 **What is the passage mainly about?**

a. what women today think of marriage
b. marriage from the past to the future
c. the average age when women get married
d. the various factors considered in marriage
e. the nuclear family and its gradual disappearance

2 **Which is closest in meaning to the word "outweigh"?**

a. scale
b. gain
c. climb
d. cancel
e. surpass

3 **What can be inferred from the passage?**

a. Women have achieved equal rights with men in the workforce.
b. Today, men value career achievement more than women.
c. Marriage based on love was crucial in medieval times.
d. Marrying more than once was not acceptable in the past.
e. Marriage will probably disappear within 50 years from now.

4 **What is the purpose of the passage?**

a. to give a good model of marriage
b. to discuss the average age to marry
c. to encourage people to marry at an older age
d. to explain about changing marriage customs
e. to compare marriage custom between the past and the future

5 **Which best fits in the blanks?**

> The average marriage age has increased due to people's preference for
> _____ their education first and finding a steady job. Extended lifespan
> might also change the _____ of marriage in the future.

a. expecting, condition
d. completing, definition
b. initiating, couple
e. aspiring, age
c. changing, interest

Unit Review

A Words

A1. Fill in the blank according to the definition.

dominate	glamorous	adoption	noble	encourage

1 _____: acting in an honest and brave way which other people admire
2 _____: to control something or someone usually in a negative way
3 _____: charmingly attractive; full of adventure and excitement
4 _____: to give someone the confidence to do something well
5 _____: the act of making a child legally part of your family

A2. Choose the most appropriate word for each blank.

1 In this dictionary there are many _____ for the word "genuine."
   a. standards　　　b. adaptations　　　c. productions　　　d. definitions

2 The family has very high _____ for their musically-talented daughters.
   a. experience　　　b. privacy　　　c. aspirations　　　d. difference

3 The benefits of opening the financial sector to foreign competition _____ the
   negative aspects.
   a. eliminate　　　b. achieve　　　c. outweigh　　　d. surrender

4 The two companies agreed to _____ their contract for another year.
   a. extend　　　b. predict　　　c. relate　　　d. shorten

5 Though engine trouble was an important factor, the _____ one was pilot error.
   a. considerable　　　b. primary　　　c. subordinate　　　d. average

A3. Complete each sentence with one of the words from the box.

legal	statistics	adopted	relatively	orphanages

1 _____ show that only 13 percent of Americans have a passport.
2 The number of _____ grew significantly after the earthquake of 2005.
3 They hope that their _____ son would someday know his biological parents.
4 Her question was a(n) _____ easy one for Professor Johns, an expert in biology.
5 He got into _____ trouble when he overstayed his visa and then lost all his
   papers.

B Expressions and Phrases

B1. Fill in the blank using an expression from the box.

previous to	due to	according to	more or less

1 _____ this cookbook, we have to roast the chicken for 50 minutes.

2 _____ her present employment, Jennifer was a promising professional golfer.

3 You've been driving for five hours straight _____. I think you need a break.

4 Flight 450, which took off smoothly, began to shake violently _____ turbulence.

**B2. Complete each sentence with an expression from the reading passages.
(Change the form of the verb if necessary.)**

take the lead	look at	consist of	do away with

1 _____ those dark clouds rolling in! I think it is going to rain.

2 The new rock band _____ two guitarists, a singer, and a drummer.

3 In order to win the championship, the captain has to step up and _____.

4 Parents insist that school teachers should _____ physical punishment of their students.

C Summary

Complete the summary with the appropriate words and expressions.

trend	average	employment	adopting
married	distant	rapidly	changing

The traditional definition of family is _____. A(n) _____ couple who has kids is just one definition. More couples, even single parents and unmarried couples are _____ children and redefining the family. Famous couples like Angelina Jolie and Brad Pitt, and single moms like Madonna are leading this _____. This is good news for children all around the world.

Marriage and its definition is changing _____. Falling in love and marrying is a relatively recent concept. Also, the _____ marriage age is gradually rising. This is because people think education and stable _____ are more important than marriage. Some sociologists expect big changes in the way people are married in the not so _____ future.

Language learning is
a part of your journey to academic success.

Fear is the main source of superstition,
and one of the main sources of cruelty.
To conquer fear is the beginning of wisdom.

Bertrand Russell

원서 술술 읽는

Smart
Reading

정답 및 해설

넥서스영어교육연구소 지음

2

✓ 고급 장문 독해 훈련
✓ 흥미 있고 유익한 32개 주제
✓ 내신, 수능, TOEFL 대비
✓ WORD BOOK 제공
✓ 무료 MP3 다운로드
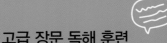 www.nexusEDU.kr

NEXUS Edu

원서 술술 읽는
Smart Reading

정답 및 해설

넥서스영어교육연구소 지음

2

NEXUS Edu

○ 정답

1. e 2. c 3. d 4. d 5. reindeer husbandry

○ 해석

스웨덴 북부, 노르웨이, 핀란드, 러시아의 콜라 반도에 거주하는 사미 족은 유럽 최대의 토착 민족 중 하나이다. 사미 족이 거주하는 대부분의 지역은 북극권 너머에 있는데, 그곳은 길고 추운 겨울로 알려진 혹독한 곳이다. 사미 족은 유목민으로서 그들 문화의 주요 특징은 순록 방목이다. 최근 일부 전문가들은 사미 족과 순록 방목과의 유대가 3만 년 전까지 거슬러 올라간다고 주장한다.

기나긴 겨울 동안에는 식량과 기타 생활필수품이 부족했다. 그 결과, 사미 족은 순록의 모든 부위를 활용하는 방법을 찾게 되었다. 순록은 살아 있는 동안에 교통수단으로 쓰이고 또한 우유를 제공하기도 했다. 일단 도살된 순록의 모든 부위는 식용으로 쓰이거나 특정 방식으로 사용되었다. 특히나 순록의 내장은 다른 곳에서 얻을 수 없는 비타민을 제공했기 때문에 중요시되었다. 사미 족은 순록의 일부 신체 부위를 자신들이 생활하는 원뿔 모양의 텐트인 라보톡을 꿰매 붙이는 데 예나 지금이나 사용하고 있다. 오늘날 스칸디나비아인들 사이에서 순록 고기는 매우 인기가 있다. 순록 소테는 그 중에서 가장 인기 있는 요리에 속한다. 순록의 뿔까지도 수입 공급원이 된다. 순록의 뿔은 가루로 곱게 빻아져 영양 보조제로 인기를 끌고 있는 아시아 국가에 수출된다.

사미 족은 현대 사회에 적응해 왔지만, 순록 방목업은 그들에게 여전히 중요하다. 활발하게 순록 목축업에 종사하는 2,800명을 포함한 전체 인구의 약 10%의 사미 족이 순록 목축업과 관련된 일을 하고 있다. 많은 지역에서 순록을 방목하는 가문의 혈통을 입증할 수 있는 사미 족만이 순록을 합법적으로 소유하고 사육할 수 있다.

많은 전통 산업과 마찬가지로 순록 목축업도 석유 탐사와 지구 온난화의 폭넓은 영향을 비롯한 많은 원인들로부터 위협을 받고 있다. 그럼에도 사미 족은 민족의 문화 정체성을 대표하는 이 중요한 특색을 유지하기 위해 부단히 노력하고 있다.

○ 해설

1 이 글의 주요 내용은 무엇인가?
 a. 북유럽 국가의 거주민들
 b. 사미 족의 유목 생활방식
 c. 스칸디나비아 인과 그들의 순록 활용
 d. 현대 사회에서 사미 족이 직면한 문제
 e. 사미 족과 순록의 밀접한 유대관계

2 "scarce"의 뜻에 가장 가까운 단어는 무엇인가?
 a. 차가운
 b. 덮인
 c. 충분하지 않은
 d. 풍부한
 e. 중대한

3 빈칸에 들어갈 가장 적절한 단어는 무엇인가?
 a. ~ 대신에
 b. 결국에
 c. 더욱이
 d. 그럼에도 불구하고
 e. 게다가

4 다음 중 사실은 무엇인가?
 a. 사미 족은 남부 유럽에 위치한 나라들에서 살고 있다.
 b. 순록 고기는 인기가 많아 아시아 국가에 수출된다.
 c. 사미 족이라면 누구나 순록을 법적으로 소유하고 목축할 수 있다.
 d. 사미 족은 순록 산업을 지키기 위해 애쓰고 있다.
 e. 사미 족이 유럽에 정착한 것은 그리 오래되지 않았다.

5 "this key characteristic"이 가리키는 것은 무엇인가?

○ 구문해설

1행_ Inhabiting northern Sweden, Norway, Finland, and the Kola Peninsula of Russia, the Sami are one of the largest indigenous groups in Europe.
⇒ Inhabiting northern Sweden, Norway, Finland, and the Kola Peninsula of Russia는 분사구문으로 의미상의 주어는 the Sami이다.

2행_ Much of the area they live in is above the Arctic Circle—a harsh environment known for long, cold winters.
⇒ the area와 they 사이에 관계대명사가 생략되었으며, 문장의 주어는 Much of the area이다. a harsh environment와 known 사이에 「관계대명사+be동사」가 생략되었다고 생각하면 문장 구조를 쉽게 이해할 수 있다.

10행_ The reindeer intestines were particularly important since they provided vitamins that were unavailable elsewhere.
⇒ since는 접속사로 이유를 나타내며, that은 관계대명사로 선행사는 important vitamins이다.

23행_ Like many traditional industries, reindeer husbandry is under threat from a number of sources, including oil exploration and the wider effects of global warming.
⇒ Like는 전치사로 '~처럼'이라는 의미이다. including 또한 전치사로 '~을 포함하여'라는 의미이며, excluding은 반대의 뜻을 가지고 있다.

UNIT 1-2 First to the Americas

Pre-reading Activity

1. F 2. F 3. T

정답

1. d 2. d 3. a 4. b 5. e

해석

1만 5,000년 전에 아시아로부터 건너와 현재의 아메리카 대륙에 정착한 사람들을 어떻게 부를 수 있을까? 이들을 가리키는 명칭으로 아메리카 원주민, 퍼스트 네이션, 미국 토착민, 아메리칸 인디언, 또는 단순히 인디언이 있다. 미국 원주민의 일부 부족을 대상으로 실시한 최근 여론 조사에서는 아메리칸 인디언이 1위를 차지했다.

유럽인의 후손인 많은 미국인들은 원주민을 가리키는 정확한 명칭을 생각해 내려 애쓰는 데 반해, 대부분의 고대 정착민들은 그 논쟁을 재미있어 한다. 그저 간단히 말하자면 그들은 어떤 명칭으로 불리든 신경 쓰지 않는다. 실제로 미국 남서부의 나바호 부족, 동부 캐나다의 이로쿼이, 중앙아메리카의 올멕 부족을 비롯해서 수천에 이르는 다양한 부족이 아메리카 대륙 전역에 분포해 있다. 이는 빙산의 일각에 불과하다.

오늘날 대부분의 과학자들은 이런 고대 여행자들이 시베리아를 지나 베링 육교를 거쳐 알래스카를 통해 캐나다와 미국으로 간 후, 중앙아메리카를 지나 남아메리카의 최남단에 도달했다고 생각한다. 일부 초기 방랑자들은 계속해서 남하했지만, 일부는 한 장소에 천막을 치고 정착했다.

페루에서 발견된 잉카인 미라의 DNA에 대한 최근 유전적 연구에서 잉카인들이 아시아인과 밀접한 관계가 있다는 사실이 밝혀졌다. 또 다른 흥미로운 사실은 대부분의 미국 원주민에게 푸른 몽고반점이 있다는 점이다.

15세기 후반의 유럽인의 도착은 토착민에게 유쾌한 일이 아니었다. 아메리카 대륙 전역에 많이 분포해 있던 인구는 유럽 식민지화로 야기된 질병, 전쟁, 대량학살 등으로 줄어들었다. 미국 원주민의 수는 미국이 스페인, 영국, 프랑스 등의 식민지가된 후 첫 2세기 동안 급격하게 감소했다. 특히 천연두라는 한 질병으로 매사추세츠 주에서만 미국 원주민의 90%가 사망했다.

해설

1 마지막 문단의 주요 내용은 무엇인가?
   a. 유럽이 아메리카 대륙을 식민지화한 동기
   b. 유럽인들의 공격에서 살아남은 여러 부족
   c. 아메리카 원주민 사이에 퍼졌던 질병
   d. 유럽인의 도착으로 많은 인디언이 죽게 된 경우
   e. 아메리카 대륙에 처음 발을 디딘 사람들이 유럽인의 이주에 맞선 방식

2 밑줄 친 "the tip of the iceberg"의 뜻은 무엇인가?
   a. 단서, 비결, 인용의 열거
   b. 쉽게 할 수 있는 것
   c. 본색을 감추는 것
   d. 좀 더 크거나 복잡한 것의 일부
   e. 다루기에 논란의 여지가 많고 예민한 문제

3 빈칸에 들어갈 가장 적절한 말은 무엇인가?
   a. 다른 방랑자는 계속 남쪽으로 향했지만
   b. 다른 방랑자는 고국으로 돌아가기 시작했지만
   c. 유럽인들은 그들을 미국 인디언이라 불렀지만
   d. 남아메리카가 유럽인에게 침략 당했지만
   e. 유럽인이 계속 아메리카 대륙으로 왔지만

4 "decimated"의 뜻에 가장 가까운 단어는 무엇인가?
   a. 해산되었다
   b. 학살당했다
   c. 보존되었다
   d. 진단받았다
   e. 정복되었다

5 이 글에서 유추할 수 있는 내용은 무엇인가?
   a. 아메리카 대륙에는 아시아 사람들이 도착하기 오래 전부터 몇몇 부족들이 살고 있었다.
   b. 아메리카 대륙에 처음 온 사람들은 남아메리카의 최남단까지 가지 못했다.
   c. 고대 여행자들은 매우 커다란 배를 사용해서 아메리카 대륙으로 이동했다.
   d. 남아메리카에 살던 미국 인디언은 북부로 이주했다.
   e. 대부분의 아메리카 원주민은 유럽인이 들여온 질병의 항체를 갖고 있지 않았다.

구문해설

4행_ In a recent poll among some tribes of Native Americans in the United States, it was found that *American Indians* came out on top.

　　　　　　　　　　가주어 　　　　진주어

6행_ While many Americans of European descent try to figure out what the correct label for the indigenous people is, most of the ancient settlers get a kick out of the discussion.

⇒ While은 접속사로 주절과 반대·비교·대조를 나타내어 '그런데, 한편으로는'라는 의미이다. what the correct label for the indigenous people is 는 명사절로 figure out의 목적어 역할을 하고 있다.

18행_ Another interesting fact is that most Native Americans have the Mongolian blue birthmark.

⇒ that은 접속사로 명사절을 이끌며, 주격 보어 역할을 하고 있다.

21행_ Populations that were huge across the Americas were decimated due to disease, warfare, and genocide brought about by the European colonization.

⇨ that은 주격 관계대명사로 선행사는 문장의 주어인 populations이다. genocide와 brought 사이에는 「관계대명사+be동사」가 생략되었다고 생각하면 문장 구조를 쉽게 이해할 수 있다.

UNIT 2-1 The Deepest Mine in the World

◉ Pre-reading Activity

valuable, potential, environment

◉ 정답

1. c 2. a 3. e 4. e 5. to clear out toxic fumes

◉ 해석

남아프리카의 요하네스버그에서 70킬로미터 떨어진 곳에 위치한 골드 필드라는 이름의 회사는 지하 4킬로미터에 이를 광산을 뚫고 있다. 작업이 완료되면 이곳은 세계에서 가장 깊은 광산이 될 것이다. 반면, 역시 남아프리카에 자리한 타우토나 광산의 깊이는 2008년에 거의 3.9킬로미터에 달해 이로써 세계에서 가장 깊은 광산이 되었다. 이러한 지나친 채광은 말 그대로 새로운 골드러시의 일부로, 회사들은 값이 계속 오르는 귀중한 금속을 찾아 광산을 깊이 파 들어가는 위험을 무릅쓰고 있다. 금은 장신구에서부터 항공기와 우주선의 전기 시스템에 이르기까지 온갖 용도로 사용되는 귀중한 금속으로써, 현재 온스당 1천 달러를 웃도는 금액에 거래되고 있다. 이렇게 금값이 올라가자 회사들은 과거에는 채굴하기에 너무 깊고 비용이 많이 들었던 금을 채굴하고 있다. 타우토나 광산에서 최근에 발견된 가장 깊은 지역에는 850만 온스의 금이 매장되어 있으리라 추정되고, 지표면에서 한 시간 가량 가야 닿을 수 있는 깊이에 있다. 약 5,600명에 이르는 광부들이 지하 세계에서 값비싼 금을 끌어올리기 위해 일하고 있다.

이런 깊이에서의 금을 채굴하는 작업은 매우 위험하다. 지표면에서 이토록 깊게 들어간 광산 바닥의 공기 온도는 섭씨 60도에 이를 수 있다. 광부들의 안전한 작업을 위해 가동하는 에어컨의 크기와 동력은 어마어마하다. 채굴 작업에 사용되는 중장비와 폭발에서 발생하는 유독 가스를 제거하려면 환기 또한 매우 중요하다. 이렇게 예방 조치를 취해도 깊은 광산에서의 작업은 여전히 위험하다. 이처럼 깊은 곳에서 작업하는 타우토나와 기타 광산에서는 매년 사망자가 발생하고 있다.

세계에서 가장 깊은 광산을 운영하는 것은 위험하고 비용이 많

이 드는 사업이다. 하지만, 이미 채굴된 금의 양이 줄어들고 금값은 계속 올라가고 있으므로 앞으로 남은 유일한 방법은 아래로 내려가는 길뿐인 듯하다.

◉ 해설

1 세 번째 문단의 주요 내용은 무엇인가?
  a. 광산 개발의 필요성
  b. 사고 예방을 위한 여러 조치
  c. 광부에게 매우 위험한 작업 환경
  d. 이렇게 깊은 광산에서 발생하는 비극적 죽음
  e. 남아프리카에서의 안전시설의 중요성

2 "extract"의 뜻에 가장 가까운 단어는 무엇인가?
  a. 골라내다
  b. 파괴하다
  c. 포함하다
  d. 추정하다
  e. 억제하다

3 빈칸에 들어갈 가장 적절한 단어는 무엇인가?
  (A)
  a. 그러나
  b. 그러므로
  c. 결과적으로
  d. 예를 들어
  e. 한편

4 다음 중 사실이 아닌 것은 무엇인가?
  a. 기업은 금을 찾기 위해 위험을 무릅쓴다.
  b. 금은 다양한 범위에서 산업 용도로 사용되고 있다.
  c. 금값이 올라가서 광부들은 금을 찾기 위해 더 깊은 곳으로 내려간다.
  d. 타우토나 광산에서 가장 깊은 지역의 온도가 매우 높다.
  e. 안전 조치 덕분에 깊은 광산에서 일하는 것은 더 이상 위험하지 않다.

5 지하 광산의 공기를 정화해야 하는 이유는 무엇인가?

◉ 구문해설

4행_ When completed, it will be the world's deepest mine.

⇨ When completed는 분사구문으로, When the mine is completed로 바꿔 쓸 수 있다.

12행_ Gold, a precious metal used in everything from jewelry to the electrical systems of airplanes and spacecrafts, now trades at well over 1,000 U.S. dollars per ounce.

⇨ a precious metal ~ spacecrafts는 Gold와 동격을 이루고 있으며, 본동사는 trades이다.

14행_ With gold prices this high, companies are now mining deposits of the metal (that were once too deep and expensive to extract).

⇒ that은 주격 관계대명사로 선행사는 형용사절의 주어가 were인 것으로 보아 deposits이라는 것을 알 수 있다. 「too+형용사/부사+to부정사」는 '너무 ~해서 …할 수 없다'라는 뜻이다.

17행_ Nearly 5,600 miners work there, laboring to bring the precious gold up from this underworld.

⇒ laboring to bring the precious gold up from this underworld는 분사구문으로 의미상의 주어는 Nearly 5,600 miners이다.

26행_ Operating the deepest mine in the world is a risky and expensive business, but with shallower deposits of gold already mined and the price of gold ever rising, it seems the only way to go is down.

⇒ 동명사구가 주어 역할을 하고 있다. gold와 already, 그리고 gold와 ever 사이에 각각 「관계대명사+be동사」가 생략되었다고 생각하면 문장 구조를 쉽게 이해할 수 있다. seems와 the only way 사이에는 접속사 that이 생략되었다.

UNIT 2-2　An Underground Everest

○ 정답

1. b　2. b　3. e　4. d　5. the Voronya Cave

○ 해석

그루지야 지방의 카프카스 산맥에 있는 보로냐 동굴은 세계에서 가장 깊은 동굴이다. 보로냐 동굴은 깊이가 2천 미터 이상으로 바닥에 닿기가 어려운 것으로 밝혀졌다. 그루지야의 한 동굴 탐험가가 60미터 가량의 짧은 탐험을 했던 1960년대 초 이전에는 누구도 동굴에 들어가 본 적이 없을 정도였다.

1982년에 키예프 출신의 우크라이나 동굴 탐험팀이 동굴의 더 깊은 곳까지 탐험하기 위해 막혀 있던 동굴을 파 들어가기 시작했다. 탐험가들은 결국 1987년까지 340미터를 내려갔다. 하지만, 더 이상의 동굴 탐험이 어렵다는 사실을 깨달았다. 아무것도 없는 막다른 곳에 다다랐고, 얼음으로 뒤덮인 폭포가 있었으며, 얼음처럼 차가운 물이 지하 강으로 콸콸 쏟아져 내려가고 있었다. 게다가 틈이 너무 비좁아 통과할 수 없었을 뿐만 아니라, 탐험가들이 볼 수 없는 어둠 속으로 끝없이 이어지는 수백 미터의 수직 경사면과 수갱(수직굴)이 있었다. 더욱이 그 지역은 1992년에 발생한 정치적 분쟁과 인종 갈등이 1998년까지 안정되지 않아 동굴 탐험은 미뤄져야 했다.

마침내 2000년대에 '심연의 부름'이라 불리는 일련의 탐험대가 좁은 틈을 폭파해 수 톤에 달하는 장비와 기구를 로프에 묶어 지상으로부터 운반하면서 체계적인 동굴 탐험을 시작했다.

56명으로 구성된 탐험대는 1,840미터의 깊이에 도달하는 데 4주가 걸렸다. 뒤이어 9명으로 구성된 팀은 2004년 10월에 2,000미터가 넘는 지하 공간에 도달했고, 그곳에 '게임 오버'라는 이름을 붙였다.

동굴 탐험가들은 이것을 지하 세계의 에베레스트 산에 비유했다. 아직 보로냐 동굴 탐험을 마친 사람은 아무도 없다. 탐험대 지도자는 이렇게 말했다. "동굴을 탐험할 때는 최종 한계가 어디인지 알지 못한다. 지금도 우리가 한계에 도달했는지 아니면 탐험이 계속될지 알 수 없다. 하지만, 결국은 더 깊은 곳을 탐험하게 되리라 확신한다."

○ 해설

1 이 글의 주요 내용은 무엇인가?
　a. 보로냐 동굴에서의 조사 결과
　b. 보로냐 동굴로의 계속되는 탐험
　c. 그루지야의 사회적 정치적 갈등
　d. 보로냐 동굴과 에베레스트 산의 비교
　e. 동굴 탐험가들이 보로냐 동굴 탐험을 중단한 이유

2 "systematically"의 뜻에 가장 가까운 단어는 무엇인가??
　a. 불규칙하게
　b. 체계적으로
　c. 일관성 없게
　d. 예측할 수 없게
　e. 민감하게

3 다음 문장이 들어갈 가장 적절한 곳은 어디인가?

　2킬로미터가 넘는 깊이의 동굴이 탐험된 것은 이번이 최초였다.

4 빈칸에 들어갈 가장 적절한 단어는 무엇인가?

　지하 세계의 에베레스트 산으로 불리는 보로냐 동굴의 깊이를 추정하기는 힘들다. 하지만, 동굴 탐험가들은 많은 역경에도 불구하고 지하 세계로의 모험을 계속 감행하고 있다.

　a. 조사하기는, 방문을
　b. 상상하기는, 해석을
　c. 자리잡기는, 살기를
　d. 추정하기는, 모험을
　e. 구별하기는, 들어가기를

5 "it"이 가리키는 것은 무엇인가?

○ 구문해설

3행_ It was not even entered until the early 1960s,

⇒ It was not even entered until the early 1960s는 '1960년대가 되어서야 들어가게 되었다'라는 의미이다. until은 부정어와 함께 '~이 되어서야 비로소 …하다'라는 뜻이다.

8행_ There were dead ends <u>that</u> led nowhere, icy waterfalls, and floods <u>pouring</u> freezing water into underground rivers.

⇨ that은 주격 관계대명사로 선행사는 dead ends이다. pouring은 현재분사로 floods를 후치 수식하고 있다.

15행_ Finally, in the 2000s, a series of expeditions named "the Call of the Abyss" began systematically exploring the cave, <u>blasting through the narrow squeezes and hauling tons of gear and equipment down on ropes from the surface.</u>

⇨ blasting ~ the surface는 분사구문으로 의미상의 주어는 a series of expeditions이다.

17행_ A 56-member team spent four weeks reaching a depth of 1,840 meters, <u>followed by</u> a nine-person team <u>that</u> reached <u>a chamber</u> <u>they</u> named "Game Over" more than 2,000 meters down in October, 2004.

⇨ followed by는 '~에 뒤이어, 잇달아'라는 의미이며 주로 명사(구)와 함께 쓰인다. that은 주격 관계대명사로 선행사는 a nine-person team이다. a chamber와 they 사이에 목적격 관계대명사가 생략되었다.

UNIT 3-1　El Castillo: The Castle Pyramid

◎ 정답

1. b　2. d　3. b　4. a　5. the amazing shadows cast by the sculpture

◎ 해석

치첸 이차는 멕시코의 유카탄 반도에 자리한 주요 고고학적 유적지이다. 기원전 7세기로 거슬러 올라가 이곳은 고대 마야 문명의 가장 중요한 도시 중 한 곳으로 여겨진다. 현재 유네스코 세계 문화유산인 치첸 이차는 인기 있는 관광지이다. 이곳에는 수많은 석조 건물과 아름답게 복원된 건물들이 많이 있다. 이 정착지에는 '성(城)'을 뜻하는 스페인어 '엘 까스띠오'로 종종 불리는 쿠쿨칸 사원이 중앙에 우뚝 솟아 있다.

엘 까스띠오는 계단식 피라미드의 훌륭한 예(例)이다. 그 피라미드의 형태는 사면으로 되어 있고 각 면에는 꼭대기의 사원까지 이어지는 계단이 있다. 각각의 계단은 91단으로 이뤄져 있다. 꼭대기에 있는 단을 더하면 일 년의 일수인 365개가 된다. 이 숫자는 '합'이라 불리는 마야 달력의 일부와 일치한다. 건축물은 꼭대기에 있는 6미터 높이의 사원을 포함해서 30미터이다. 북쪽 계단에는 경사면을 타고 내려오는 깃털 달린 뱀 형상의 화

려한 조각상이 있다. 사원의 명칭인 쿠쿨칸은 실제로 깃털 달린 뱀을 뜻하는 단어로 마야 신화에서 중요한 신이었다.

춘분이나 추분에 이곳을 찾는 관광객은 그 조각이 드리우는 놀라운 그림자를 볼 수 있다. 전체 건축물은 9층으로 이루어져 있다. 고고학자들은 이것이 마야의 '지하 세계'에 아홉 단계가 있다는 마야의 우주론적 신념과 관계가 있을 것이라 생각한다. 피라미드의 중앙 계단은 13층으로 이뤄져 있다. 전문가들은 이것이 마야의 '지상 세계'의 단계 개수를 가리킨다는 데 의견을 같이 한다.

엘 까스띠오는 놀라운 건축미로 인해 멕시코에서 관광객이 두 번째로 많이 찾는 고고학적 유적지이다. 2007년에 전 세계적으로 실시한 투표에서 '신세계(新世界) 7대 불가사의' 중 한 곳으로 선정되었다.

◎ 해설

1 두 번째 문단의 주요 내용은 무엇인가?
　a. 계단식 피라미드의 다양한 예시
　b. 엘 까스띠오의 모양과 구조
　c. 마야 신화에 나오는 뱀을 뜻하는 신
　d. 마야의 달력 체계인 합
　e. 엘 까스띠오에 대한 역사적 고찰

2 "corresponds"의 뜻에 가장 가까운 단어는 무엇인가?
　a. 포함하다
　b. 수정하다
　c. 교환하다
　d. 일치하다
　e. 고수하다

3 빈칸에 들어갈 가장 적절한 단어는 무엇인가?
　a. 결합하다
　b. 나타내다
　c. 자극하다
　d. 공급하다
　e. 엉키게 하다

4 엘 까스띠오에 대한 내용 중 사실이 아닌 것은 무엇인가?
　a. 엘 까스띠오는 다른 조각상에 둘러싸여 있지 않다.
　b. 엘 까스띠오는 아홉 개의 층과 사면으로 뻗은 계단으로 이루어져 있다.
　c. 엘 까스띠오는 멕시코에서 매우 인기 있는 고고학적 유적지이다.
　d. 엘 까스띠오는 신세계 7대 불가사의에 속한다.
　e. 엘 까스띠오는 마야의 우주론적 신념과 관계가 있을 것이다.

5 춘분이나 추분에 쿠쿨칸 사원을 찾아가면 목격할 수 있는 것은 무엇인가?

7행_ The settlement is dominated by the Temple of Kukulkan, or as it is often called "El Castillo," which is Spanish for "the Castle," at its center.

⇨ as it is often called "El Castillo"는 '종종 El Castillo라고 불려지는'이라고 해석하며, which는 주격 관계대명사로 선행사는 El Castillo이다.

15행_ On the north staircase there are spectacular sculptures of feathered serpents running down the sides.

⇨ running은 현재분사로 feathered serpents를 후치 수식하고 있다.

18행_ Tourists may experience the amazing shadows cast by the sculptures, if they pay a visit during the spring or autumn equinox.

⇨ cast는 과거분사로 the amazing shadows를 후치 수식하고 있으며, 접속사 if는 조건절을 이끌고 있다.

20행_ Archeologists believe that this may be linked to the Mayan cosmological belief that there are nine levels in the Mayan "Underworld."

⇨ 두 개의 that 모두 접속사이다. 첫 번째 that은 동사 believe의 목적어를 이끌고 있다. 두 번째 that은 동격절을 이끌어 the Mayan cosmological belief를 보충 설명하고 있다.

UNIT 3-2　The Hanging Gardens of Babylon

● Pre-reading Activity

1. F　2. T　3. T

● 정답

1. e　2. c　3. b　4. a　5. d

● 해석

바빌론의 공중 정원은 현대 이라크가 자리한 곳에 있었다. 바빌론의 공중 정원은 원조 고대 세계 7대 불가사의의 하나로 기원전 600년경 한 바빌론 왕에 의해 지어졌다. 바빌론 왕이 페르시아라 불리는 다른 지역 출신의 여성과 결혼했다는 설(說)이 있다. 불행하게도 새 왕비는 향수병을 몹시 앓았다. 모든 여성이 원하는 부(富)를 소유했지만, 왕비는 자신의 모국인 페르시아를 그리워했다.

당시 바빌론은 오늘날과 마찬가지로 건조하고 황폐했다. 왕비는 나무 냄새, 각양각색의 꽃의 향기, 과일나무가 풍기는 맛있는 향과 예쁜 꽃을 그리워했다. 슬픔에 빠진 여왕을 기쁘게 하려고 왕은 세계에서 가장 아름답고 향기로운 정원을 만들겠다는 생각을 하게 되었다. 그가 페르시아의 아름다운 향을 풍기는 정원을 만든다면 왕비는 틀림없이 향수병을 극복할 수 있으리라 생각했다.

왕이 세운 공중 정원은 그 지역을 찾는 여행객들을 놀라게 했다. 공중 정원의 구조물은 매우 높았다. 정원은 줄이나 밧줄에 실제로 매달려 있지는 않았을 것이다. 공중 정원은 지구라트(고대 바빌로니아와 아시리아의 피라미드형 신전)의 일부인 테라스에 지어졌고, 유프라테스 강으로부터 물을 댔다. 왕은 특별한 기술을 사용해서 정원까지 물을 높이 끌어올렸다. 고대 그리스 역사학자들은 정원의 구조를 철저히 기록했다. 그들은 정원을 보호하기 위해 세운 벽의 두께가 10미터나 된다고 기록했다. 더욱이 정원이 매우 높은 곳에 지어졌을 때 그곳을 둘러볼 수 있는 계단과 길이 많았다.

증거 문서가 부족해서 공중 정원이 실제 창작품인지 시적인 창작품인지에 대해 논란이 일고 있다. 공중 정원의 유일한 흔적은 고대 문서에 남아 있는 수많은 이야기들이다. 또한 그림과 설계도도 수없이 많다. 과연 공중 정원은 시인에 의해 쓰여지고 화가에 의해 그려진 전설일 뿐일까?

● 해설

1 이 글의 주요 내용은 무엇인가?
　a. 왕비가 향수병을 앓도록 하려는 왕의 시도
　b. 바빌론에 살았던 한 왕비의 비참한 삶
　c. 한 바빌론 왕과 왕비에 대한 그의 헌신
　d. 여행객들의 눈길을 끌기 위해 바빌론에 지어진 멋진 정원
　e. 한 바빌론 왕이 왕비를 위해 지은 아름다운 구조물

2 "barren"의 뜻에 가장 가까운 단어는 무엇인가?
　a. 몹시 추운
　b. 비옥한
　c. 황량한
　d. 효력이 있는
　e. 변덕스러운

3 빈칸에 들어갈 가장 적절한 말은 무엇인가?
　a. 그의 땅을 비옥하게 만들려고
　b. 슬퍼하는 왕비를 기쁘게 해주려고
　c. 페르시아의 비옥한 땅을 약탈하려고
　d. 치명적인 병에 대한 치료법을 찾으려고
　e. 바빌론 제국의 힘을 키우려고

4 이 글에서 유추할 수 있는 내용은 무엇인가?
　a. 바빌론에는 비가 거의 내리지 않는다.
　b. 공중 정원은 단순히 신화나 전설에 불과하다.
　c. 왕은 페르시아를 침략해서 차지할 것이다.
　d. 공중 정원은 왕비의 향수병을 더욱 악화시켰다.
　e. 유프라테스 강에서 물을 끌어올리기 위해 많은 사람들이 동원되었다.

바빌론의 공중 정원은 향수병에 걸린 왕비를 <u>위로하려던</u> 한 바빌론의 왕에 의해 세워졌다. 나무와 꽃이 테라스에 심어졌고, 공중 정원에 있는 식물에 <u>물을 주기</u> 위해 유프라테스 강이 이용되었다.

a. 기쁘게 하려던, 죽이기

b. 도망가려던, 뿌리기

c. 놀라게 하려던, 벌목하기

d. 위로하려던, 물을 주기

e. 결혼하려던, 재배하기

구문해설

3행_ The story goes that the king married a woman from another land called Persia.

⇒ The story goes that ~은 '~라는 이야기가 있다'는 뜻으로, 접속사 that은 생략할 수도 있다.

5행_ Though she had <u>all the riches</u> <u>any woman</u> could want, she longed for her native land of Persia.

⇒ all the riches와 any woman 사이에 목적격 관계대명사가 생략되었다. long for는 '~을 갈망하다'라는 의미이다.

7행_ The land of Babylon was dry and barren — exactly <u>like</u> it is today.

⇒ like는 접속사로 '~와 똑같이, ~처럼'이라는 의미이다.

13행_ The Hanging Gardens <u>that</u> the king built <u>shocked</u> travelers to the area.

⇒ that은 목적격 관계대명사로 주어 The Hanging Gardens를 수식하는 형용사절을 이끌고 있으며, 문장의 본동사는 shocked이다.

15행_ They were built on terraces <u>which</u> were part of the ziggurat and were irrigated by <u>water</u> <u>lifted up</u> from the Euphrates.

⇒ which는 주격 관계대명사로 선행사는 terraces이다. water와 lifted up 사이에 「관계대명사+be동사」가 생략되었다고 생각하면 문장 구조를 쉽게 이해할 수 있다.

24행_ The only remains of the gardens are the numerous stories about <u>them</u> <u>that</u> are in ancient texts.

⇒ that은 주격 관계대명사로 선행사는 the numerous stories이다. them은 the gardens를 의미한다.

UNIT 4-1　Bamboo Clothing

Pre-reading Activity

plant, hardwood, incredibly, climate

정답

1. d　2. c　3. e　4. a　5. d

해석

당신이 다음에 구매할 티셔츠, 속옷, 양말, 청바지, 운동복, 블라우스의 원료는 면, 폴리에스테르, 기타 인기 있는 직물이 아닐 수도 있다. 어쩌면 대나무가 원료일지도 모른다. 대나무는 의류 산업에 새로운 친환경적인 대안으로 떠오르고 있다. 많은 패션 전문가들은 대나무 직물이 일시적으로 유행할지, 아니면 오랫동안 사용될지 궁금해 하고 있다.

개인적 소견으로는, 대나무가 계속 사용되리라고 생각한다. 대나무에는 비단 같은 천연의 광택이 있다. 대나무는 통풍이 매우 잘 되고 비교적 무거운 면직물보다 훨씬 가볍게 느껴진다. 또한 면과 기타 직물보다 피부를 끈적거리지 않게 유지시켜 주는 재료이다. 대나무는 자연적으로 자외선을 차단하므로 태양이 피부에 끼칠 수 있는 손상을 최소화하는 데 도움을 준다. 대나무가 제공하는 또 다른 건강상 이점으로 대나무에는 항균성이 있어 박테리아나 바이러스와 같은 해로운 미생물을 파괴한다는 점이다.

제품이 환경에 미치는 영향을 중요하게 생각하는 시대에서 대나무가 가진 가장 중요한 측면은 아마도 내구성일 것이다. 면과 기타 천연 직물은 기르고, 재배하고, 추수하는 데 많은 자원이 필요하다. 말할 필요도 없이 폴리에스테르와 기타 인공 직물은 환경에 악몽 같은 존재이다. 반면에 대나무는 기타 나무 식물에 비해 매우 빨리 자란다. 또한 대부분의 다른 직물보다 오래가고 완전히 유기농이기도 하다. 살충제와 제초제 같은 많은 화학물질을 거의 필요로 하지 않는다.

편안함의 관점에서 볼 때 대나무 티셔츠와 대나무로 만든 다른 의류는 입고 있는 동안 매우 부드러운 상태를 유지한다. 왜 대부분의 패션 전문가들이 직물과 의류 산업으로의 대나무의 새로운 등장에 대해 흥분하고 있는지 쉽게 알 수 있다.

해설

1 이 글의 주요 내용은 무엇인가?

a. 유기농 기법을 이용한 환경 친화적 패션

b. 의복으로 대나무와 면의 사용에 대한 이점

c. 대나무와 기타 직물의 비교

d. 환경 친화적 패션을 위한 새로운 직물인 대나무 의류

e. 대나무 직물이 환경에 미치는 긍정적 영향

2 "properties"의 뜻에 가장 가까운 단어는 무엇인가?
  a. 내용물
  b. 재료
  c. 특징
  d. 소유물
  e. 귀중품

3 다음 문장이 들어갈 가장 적절한 곳은 어디인가?

> 이런 점에서 대나무는 환경에 더 좋다.

4 다음 중 사실이 아닌 것은 무엇인가?
  a. 대나무 직물은 거칠고 변하기 쉽다.
  b. 대나무에는 자연적으로 자외선 차단 기능이 있다.
  c. 대나무에는 일부 박테리아를 죽이는 항균성이 있다.
  d. 대나무는 다른 나무 식물과 달라서 비료 없이도 빨리 자란다.
  e. 대나무는 독한 화학물질로 처리하지 않아서 대나무 의류는 건강에 좋다.

5 빈칸에 들어갈 가장 적절한 말은 무엇인가?

> 대나무 직물은 다른 직물에서 발견할 수 없는 훌륭한 <u>특징</u>이 많이 있다. 또한 대나무는 환경적으로 많은 <u>이점</u>을 지녀 혁신적인 직물로 각광받고 있다.

  a. 선택, 단점
  b. 전문가, 흥미
  c. 화학물질, 이익
  d. 특징, 이익
  e. 물건, 장애물

◑ 구문해설

1행_ The next T-shirts, underwear, socks, jeans, sweatshirts, or blouses <u>you</u> buy <u>might</u> not be made of cotton, polyester, or any other popular fabric.

➡ blouses와 you 사이에 목적격 관계대명사가 생략되었으며, might는 미래를 추측하는 의미로 쓰였다.

4행_ Many fashion experts are wondering <u>if</u> bamboo fabric will be a fad, or <u>if</u> it will be around for a long time.

➡ 접속사 if는 '~인지'의 의미로 조건절이 아닌 명사절을 이끌어 wondering의 목적어 역할을 하고 있다.

10행_ Another health benefit is <u>that</u> bamboo has antimicrobial properties <u>that</u> destroy some harmful microorganisms such as bacteria and even some viruses.

➡ 첫 번째 that은 접속사로 주격 보어 역할을 하는 명사절을 이끌고 있다. 두 번째 that은 주격 관계대명사로 선행사는 antimicrobial properties이다.

14행_ Cotton and other natural fabrics take a lot of resources to <u>grow</u>, <u>cultivate</u>, and <u>harvest</u>.

➡ grow, cultivate, harvest는 to부정사로 병렬관계를 이루고 있다.

21행_ <u>It</u> is pretty easy <u>to see why most fashion people</u> (가주어) (진주어) are excited about this new entry into the fabric and clothing industry.

UNIT 4-2　The Evolution of Clothing

◑ 정답

1. c　**2.** e　**3.** d　**4.** a　**5.** the scientific community

◑ 해석

과거에 의류는 단지 기능과 패션에 관계가 있었다. 의류의 기능은 우리를 따뜻하고 편안하게 해주기 위해 의복으로 신체를 덮는 것에 불과했다. 그리고 나서 패션은 우리를 보기 좋게 만들어 주기 위해 나타났다. 하지만, 오늘날에는 의류 산업 전체가 많은 혁신이 일어나고 있다. 이런 혁신들 중 하나는 건강에 목적을 둔다. 일부 새로운 의류 제품은 신체에 약과 같은 작용을 하도록 디자인되고 있다.

이러한 새로운 의류 제품은 어떨 것 같은가? 첫째로, 의류에 들어가는 재료가 약간 다르다. 몇몇 사람들은 건강을 증진시키는 두 종류의 광물이 있다고 주장한다. 이 광물 중 하나는 전기석(電氣石)이라 불리는 준보석이다. 또 하나는 자철석(磁鐵石)이라 불리는 회색 돌이다. 자철석은 이름으로 알 수 있듯이 지구에서 자연적으로 발생하는 자성이 가장 강한 광물이다. 또한 자철석은 논란의 여지가 있는 자기장 요법을 믿는 사람들에 의해 장신구로 널리 쓰인다. 전기석과 자철석을 몸에 지니면 전반적인 건강이 향상될 것이라고 추정하고 있다. 의심스럽다면 텔레비전을 켜고 몇몇 프로 운동선수들을 보라. 오늘날 다수의 유명한 운동선수가 이 새로운 장식이 자신의 신체 건강을 향상시켜 줄 것이라 생각해서 이런 광물을 목걸이로 착용하고 있다. 더욱이 전기석과 자철석으로 만든 팔찌, 목걸이, 기타 장신구를 착용하면 집중력이 향상된다고 주장한다.

일부 패션 디자이너들이 이런 준보석을 갈아서 의류를 만드는 직물에 넣겠다는 아이디어를 떠올린 것은 시간 문제였다. 초기 결과로 보아 장래성이 많다. 과학계는 이런 제품을 입을 때 발생하는 진정한 효과에 대해서 여전히 논쟁을 벌이지만, 고객들은 매우 좋아하는 것 같다.

1 이 글의 제목과 바꿔 쓸 수 있는 가장 적절한 것은 무엇인가?
   a. 새로운 개념의 스포츠 의류
   b. 새로운 패션의 기능
   c. 의복의 새로운 재료
   d. 최신식 환경 친화적 상품
   e. 의류 산업의 몰락

2 빈칸에 들어갈 가장 적절한 말은 무엇인가?
   a. 마음의 평안을 위한 치료법
   b. 핼러윈 파티를 위한 의상
   c. 좋았던 옛 시절에 대한 향수
   d. 극한 스포츠의 인기
   e. 신체를 위한 약품

3 "ingredients"의 뜻에 가장 가까운 단어는 무엇인가?
   a. 수량
   b. 행사
   c. 과정
   d. 구성 요소
   e. 제안

4 글쓴이가 "controversial"이라는 단어를 언급한 이유는 무엇인가?
   a. 자기장 요법의 효능에 대해 논쟁을 벌여서
   b. 자철석으로 만든 목걸이를 착용하는 운동선수들이 많아서
   c. 자철석이 건강에 좋다고 생각하는 사람들이 많아서
   d. 전기석과 자철석 중 어느 것이 더 좋은지에 대한 논쟁이 있어서
   e. 자기장 요법이 일시적인 유행이라고 믿는 사람들이 많아서

5 이 글에 따르면, 이러한 유행에 회의적인 태도를 취하는 사람은 누구인가?

● 구문해설

2행_ The function was just to cover our bodies with clothing to keep us warm and comfortable.

⇨ to cover ~ comfortable은 to부정사구로 주격 보어 역할을 한다. to keep은 '유지하기 위해'라는 뜻으로 to부정사의 부사적 용법 중 목적을 나타낸다.

10행_ First off, the ingredients going into clothes are a bit different.

⇨ First off는 '첫째로'라는 뜻이며, 현재분사 going이 명사 the ingredients를 후치 수식하고 있다.

20행_ In addition, the athletes say they have much greater concentration while wearing wristbands, necklaces, and other trinkets made of tourmaline and magnetite.

⇨ say와 they 사이에 접속사 that이 생략되었다. while wearing ~ magnetite은 while they are wearing ~으로 바꿔 쓸 수 있다.

⇨ 접속사 while은 '~하고 있는 동안에'라는 의미로 쓰였다. 종속절이 주절의 주어와 동일할 경우, 종속절의 「주어+be동사」는 생략이 가능하다.

25행_ While the scientific community still debates the true power of wearing these items, the customers seem to enjoy them very much.

⇨ 접속사 while은 주절과 반대·비교·대조를 나타내어 '그런데, 한편으로는'이라는 의미로 쓰였다.

UNIT 5-1   An Overview of Organic Farming

● 정답

1. e   2. e   3. c   4. b   5. b

● 해석

농장의 수확량과 수익성을 증가시키려면 다량의 화학물질과 살충제를 사용해야 한다. 과학자들은 막대한 양의 농작물을 재배하기 위해 곡물, 과일, 채소의 유전자를 연구하고 있다. 더욱이 가축 한 마리당 더 많은 고기를 얻으려고 농장에서 사육하는 가축에 정기적으로 인공 호르몬을 주사하고 있다. 이는 물론 가축의 건강에 영향을 미치고, 많은 사람들이 결국은 인간 소비자의 건강에도 영향을 미친다는 것을 알고 있다. 농업과 축산업에서 그토록 여러 종류의 많은 화학물질을 사용하는 것 또한 환경에 많은 해를 끼친다. 이런 문제에 대한 반응으로 유기 농업 운동이 성행하고 있다.

유기농은 유해한 화학물질 사용에 대한 해결책을 제공해 왔다. 농부가 병충해로 인해 농작물을 잃을 수는 없다. 하지만, 살충제는 아주 작은 양이더라도 소비자의 건강에 좋지 않다. 따라서 유기농에서는 대체적 방법을 사용한다. 화학물질을 살포하는 대신에 농부들은 종종 식물에 봉지를 씌운다. 또한 해충을 박멸하기 위해 천적을 사용하기도 한다. 농부들은 작은 꽃노린재, 무당벌레 등을 농장에 풀어놓는다. 유전자 변형 식물은 해충이 식물의 맛이나 질감에 더 이상 끌리지 않게 해서 해충을 박멸하는 또 다른 방법이다. 그러나 유전적으로 식물을 변형하는 것은 완전한 자연 농법을 지지하는 사람에게 여전히 논란거리가 되고 있다.

농부들은 제충국과 로테논처럼 천연자원으로 만든 살충제를 사용한다. 해충의 위협 없이 농작물을 성공적으로 재배하는 일은 매우 어렵다. 그래서 많은 농부들이 좀 더 효과적이지만 여전히 논란의 여지가 있는 방법을 선택하는 것이다.

천연 살충제를 사용하는 가장 중요한 이유는 빗물이 땅 위를 흐르는 지역의 토양과 물을 오염시킬 수 있는 유독성 살충제에 의한 환경 피해를 막기 위해서이다. 완전히 자연적인 방법은, 비용면에서 볼 때 시장 사회에 효율적이지는 않지만 유기농법에는 상당한 발전을 이루었다.

○ 해설

1 두 번째 문단의 주요 내용은 무엇인가?
a. 유독성 살충제 사용에 대한 경고
b. 유전적으로 변형된 식물에 대한 논쟁
c. 유기 농법에 사용되는 천연 살충제
d. 화학물질의 대체물로 사용되는 천적
e. 농업 분야에 사용되는 유해한 화학물질보다 안전한 대안

2 "they"가 가리키는 것은 무엇인가?
a. 화학물질
b. 대체 방법
c. 유전자 변형 식물
d. 천적
e. 해충

3 "controversial"의 뜻에 가장 가까운 단어는 무엇인가?
a. 인공적인
b. 만연하는
c. 논쟁의 여지가 있는
d. 전통적인
e. 확실한

4 다음 중 건강에 유해할 가능성이 있는 위험으로 본문에 언급되지 않은 것은 무엇인가?
a. 농작물에 화학물질과 살충제를 살포하기
b. 해충의 천적을 놓아두기
c. 가축에 인공 호르몬 주입
d. 토양과 수질을 파괴하는 유독성 살충제
e. 곡물, 과일, 채소의 유전자 조작

5 유기농에 대한 글쓴이의 태도는 무엇인가?
a. 비판적인
b. 긍정적인
c. 무관심한
d. 회의적인
e. 중립적인

○ 구문해설

3행_ In addition, <u>livestock</u> <u>raised</u> on farms are regularly injected with artificial hormones to create more meat per animal.
⇨ livestock과 raised 사이에 「관계대명사+be동사」가 생략되었다고 생각하면 문장 구조를 쉽게 이해할 수 있다.

6행_ <u>The use</u> of so many other types of chemicals in the grain and livestock industries also <u>does</u> a lot of harm to the environment.
⇨ 위 문장의 주어는 The use이며, 본동사는 does이다.

17행_ <u>modifying plants genetically</u> <u>is</u> still controversial to those who advocate a completely natural approach to farming
⇨ 동명사구(modifying plants genetically)가 주어로 쓰이는 경우에는 단수 취급을 하므로 동사는 is가 와야 한다.

20행_ It is very challenging to raise a successful crop
　　　　가주어　　　　　　　　　　　　　　　　진주어
without the threat of insect pests,

22행_ The most important reason for using natural pesticides is <u>to avoid</u> the environmental damage from toxic pesticides <u>that</u> ruin soil and water quality in regions <u>where</u> there are run-offs.
⇨ to avoid ~ run-offs는 to부정사구로 주격 보어 역할을 한다. that은 주격 관계대명사로 선행사는 toxic pesticides이다. where는 관계부사로 선행사는 regions이다.

UNIT 5-2　Economic Viability of Organic Farming

○ Pre-reading Activity

1. F　　2. T　　3. F

○ 정답

1. a　**2.** d　**3.** c　**4.** c　**5.** to allow the soil to recover its nutrient content

○ 해석

식료품 구매 고객은 전통적 방법으로 재배한 식품보다 유기농 식품의 가격이 비싸다는 사실을 분명히 알고 있다. 아마도 그들은 더 우수한 품질의 건강식품을 구매하고 있다고 믿을 것이다. 유기농 식품이 다른 식품보다 건강에 좋다는 사실이 더욱 분명해지고 있지만, 생산 방법이 더욱 비싼 것도 확실하다.

농작물을 생산하기 위해 같은 토양을 매년 사용하면 토양에서 영양분이 빠져나가므로 농부들은 종종 질산 비료로 토양을 비옥하게 만드는 인위적 방법을 사용한다. 유기농을 하는 농부들은 대개 윤작(輪作)을 이용해서 일정 기간 동안 땅을 휴지(休止)하여 토양이 영양분을 회복하게 만든다. 또한 운반비용이 더 많이 드는 거름이나 퇴비로 토양을 비옥하게 만든다.

인위적 농법을 사용하지 않는 이런 특유의 방법들은 또한 공간을 차지한다. 예를 들어, 닭을 방목해서 키우는 것보다 닭장에 가둬 키우면 비용이 더 적게 든다. 농부들은 닭에게 대량생산된 먹이를 주며 닭을 극도로 비좁은 닭장에 가두어 떠나지 못하

게 함으로써 물리적 공간의 생산성을 극대화할 수 있다. 그러나 방목해서 키운 닭이 낳는 달걀에는 닭장에 갇힌 닭이 낳는 달걀에 없는 영양분이 많다. 이는 방목해서 키운 닭이 토양에서 섭취한 음식에는 조류가 함유되어 있는데, 그것은 달걀의 형태로 섭취할 때 인간의 건강에 유익하다.

유기농은 넓은 면적의 땅이 필요하므로 식량 생산 체계에 전체적으로 적용하는 것은 불가능하다. 유기농은 상대적으로 넓은 면적의 땅에서 더 적은 생산량을 내므로 이는 간접적으로 환경에 부정적 영향을 미칠 수 있다. 유기농에 대한 의문과 그것이 주는 이로움은 여전히 남아 있으므로 더 많은 연구와 혁신이 분명히 필요하다.

○ 해설

1 이 글의 주요 내용은 무엇인가?
   a. 유기농의 장단점
   b. 유기농의 부정적 측면
   c. 토양을 비옥하게 하는 여러 가지 방법
   d. 유기농법에 숨어 있는 과학
   e. 유기농을 사용한 농작물 생산의 이점

2 "leach"의 뜻에 가장 가까운 단어는 무엇인가?
   a. 바꾸다
   b. 경작하다
   c. 황폐화시키다
   d. 소모시키다
   e. 진정시키다

3 방목해서 키운 닭에 대한 내용 중 사실이 아닌 것은 무엇인가?
   a. 그것들은 영양이 풍부한 달걀을 낳는다.
   b. 그것들은 키우고 돌보는 데 비용이 많이 든다.
   c. 그것들은 닭장에 가둬 키우는 닭보다 공간을 덜 필요로 한다.
   d. 그것들은 닭장에 갇힌 닭처럼 비좁은 공간에서 자라지 않는다.
   e. 닭을 방목해서 기르는 것은 닭을 가둬 기르는 것보다 생산량이 많다.

4 유기농에 대한 저자의 태도는 무엇인가?
   a. 그것은 환경에 끔찍한 영향을 미칠 것이다.
   b. 그것은 가까운 미래에 사라질 유행에 불과하다.
   c. 그것은 장래성이 있지만, 더 많은 작업과 연구가 필요하다.
   d. 그것은 미래에 전통적 농법을 완전히 대체할 것이다.
   e. 그것은 지나치게 비용이 많이 들고, 실행하기에 너무 많은 노동이 필요하다.

5 유기농을 하는 농부들이 윤작을 할 때 토양을 일정 기간 휴지(休止)하는 것은 무엇인가?

○ 구문해설

3행_ While it is becoming more evident that organic food
   _{가주어} ... _{진주어}
   is healthier than other food, it is also clear that the
   _{가주어}
   production methods are certainly more expensive.
   _{진주어}

8행_ Organic farmers commonly use crop rotation and allow the ground to lie for some period of time to help the soil recover its nutrient content.
⇨ 「help+목적어+동사원형」의 형태를 알아두자.

14행_ Farmers can maximize productivity of a physical space by confining hens that never leave their cages in extremely close quarters while feeding them manufactured feed
⇨ that은 주격 관계대명사로 선행사는 confining hens이다. while feeding them manufactured feed는 분사구문으로 while they(farmers) feed ~로 바꿔 쓸 수 있다.

16행_ However, free-range chickens lay eggs that contain many nutrients that their cage-produced counterparts do not.
⇨ 첫 번째 that은 주격 관계대명사로 선행사는 eggs이다. 두 번째 that은 목적격 관계대명사로 선행사는 many nutrients이다.

17행_ This is a result of allowing free-range chickens to pick food from the soil that contains algae, which is healthy for humans when delivered in the form of eggs.
⇨ 「allow+목적어+to부정사」의 문장 구조를 알아두자. when과 delivered 사이에 'algae is'가 생략되었다. that과 which는 각각 주격 관계대명사로 선행사는 the soil과 algae이다.

20행_ The amount of land that organic farming requires makes it impossible to apply to the entire food
   _{가목적어} ... _{진목적어}
   production system.

UNIT 6-1 　Absent-Minded Genius

○ 정답

1. a　2. e　3. d　4. c　5. because she spends her time in her imagination

○ 해석

1999년 미국 기억력 대회에서 우승한 타티아나 쿨리에게는 많은 칭호가 붙는다. 그것들 중 하나는 '세계에서 가장 똑똑한 미인'과 또 다른 하나는 '세계 최고의 암기자'이다. 타티아나는 몇 분 만에 100명의 얼굴과 그에 해당하는 이름을 외운다. 그녀는 한 줄로 늘어놓은 숫자 4,000개를 읽는 것만큼이나 빨리 암기할 수 있다. 그녀에게 한 줄로 늘어놓은 단어 500개를 읽게 해

보아라. 그러면 그녀는 완벽한 순서로 당신에게 다시 말해 줄 것이다.

그녀의 친구와 가족이 그녀에게 칭하는 호칭 중 하나는 '세계에서 가장 건망증이 심한 여성'이다. 타티아나는 대중들이 앞에 있는 무대에서 놀라운 암기 능력을 펼쳐 보일 수 있지만 일상생활의 일들은 기억하지 못한다. 그녀를 '포스트잇 여왕'이라 부르는 사람이 많은 것도 이런 이유에서다. 타티아나는 포스트잇을 가지고 다니면서 자신이 해야 할 일, 전화해야 할 사람, 개인 소지품을 놔둔 장소를 기록한다. 그녀의 어머니는 "타티아나는 모든 것을 잊어버려요."라고 말한다. 타티아나는 약속 장소에 나가는 것을 잊을 뿐만 아니라 약속 시간이 몇 시였는지도 기억하지 못한다. 그녀는 포스트잇에 약속에 대해 적어 놓지 않으면 도저히 약속 장소에 나가는 것을 기억하지 못할 거라 말한다. 타티아나는 암기와 매일 해야 할 일을 기억하는 것은 다른 기술이라 설명한다. 암기는 사물을 시각화하는 것이다. 예를 들어, 타티아나는 단어 500개를 암기할 때 각 단어의 이미지를 머릿속에 만들고 단어와 그 이미지를 연결한다. 일단 머릿속에 만들어 놓은 이미지를 통해 단어가 확실히 연결되면 기억하기가 쉽다. 그녀는 세계 최고의 기억술사들은 상상하는 데 시간을 보내기 때문에 세상사를 기억하는 데 어려움을 느낀다고 설명한다.

해설

1 이 글의 주요 내용은 무엇인가?
a. 타티아나의 놀라운 암기 능력과 그녀의 건망증
b. 한 줄로 늘어놓은 4,000개의 숫자를 암기하는 법
c. 타티아나의 유용한 암기 기술
d. 타티아나 쿨리의 삶과 그녀의 성공 이야기
e. 타티아나를 도와주는 똑똑한 포스트잇

2 "corresponding"의 뜻에 가장 가까운 단어는 무엇인가?
a. 집행하는
b. 예상되는
c. 일관된
d. 닮지 않은
e. 걸맞은

3 빈칸에 들어갈 가장 적절한 단어는 무엇인가?
(A)
a. ~ 이래 줄곧
b. ~ 때문에
c. ~임에도 불구하고
d. ~인 반면
e. ~처럼

4 타티아나 쿨리에 대한 내용 중 사실이 아닌 것은 무엇인가?
a. 그녀는 포스트잇 메모를 어디든지 가지고 다닌다.
b. 그녀는 잊지 않기 위해 매일 해야 할 일의 목록을 적는다.
c. 그녀는 자기 주변의 사람과 사물에 관심을 갖지 않는다.
d. 그녀는 1999년 미국 기억력 대회에서 1등을 차지했다.
e. 타티아나는 시각화와 연상이라는 두 가지 암기 기술을 사용한다.

5 타티아나가 세상사를 기억하기 힘든 이유는 무엇인가?

구문해설

5행_ Or let her read 500 words in a row.
⇨ 「let +목적어+동사원형」의 문장 구조를 알아두자.
☆ I won't let you go. (나는 당신을 보내지 않겠습니다.)

7행_ One of many other titles that her friends and family call her is "The World's Most Absent-minded Woman."
⇨ that은 목적격 관계대명사로 선행사는 many other titles이다. 주어는 One 이고 본동사는 is이다.

10행_ She carries around Post-it notes to jot down notes about things she must remember to do, people she must call, and reminders of where she put her personal belongings.
⇨ things와 she 사이에 목적격 관계대명사 which 또는 that이 생략되었다. people과 she 사이에도 목적격 관계대명사 who(m) 또는 that이 생략되었다.

19행_ when memorizing a list of 500 words, she makes mental images of each and every one of the 500 words and then connects the words and their images together
⇨ when memorizing a list of 500 words는 접속사를 동반한 분사구문으로 의미상의 주어는 she이며 when she memorizes ~로 바꿔 쓸 수 있다.

UNIT 6-2 Tricks of the Mind

정답

1. c 2. c 3. b 4. e 5. actors or stooges in his show

해석

데렌 브라운은 2000년부터 현재까지 진행한 몇몇 쇼 덕택에 영국에서 스타로 인정받고 있다. 이 쇼들은 BBC에 방송되었고 영국에서 데렌을 슈퍼스타로 만드는 데 일조했다. 데렌은 무대 최면술사로 일을 시작했다. 이는 데렌이 방청객을 골라 무대에 올라오게 하고 이상한 행동을 하도록 최면을 거는 일을 했다는 뜻이다. 예를 들어, 데렌이 "긴장을 푸시고 내가 말하는 대로 하세요."라고 말한다. 그러면 그 방청객은 일종의 최면 상태에 들어가 데렌이 말하는 것은 무엇이든지 한다. 데렌은 "내가 셋까지 세면 당신은 다시 다섯 살이 될 겁니다."라고 종종 말한다. 그리고 데렌이 "하나, 둘, 셋"하고 세면 방청객은 마치 다섯

살 때 그랬던 것처럼 말하면서 이것저것 만지고 놀며 방 이곳저
곳을 뛰어다닐 것이다.

이것이 최면술의 힘이다. 어떤 사람들은 최면에 걸리면 무슨
일이든 거의 할 수 있다. 이런 종류의 사람들이 광고회사가 좋
아하는 사람들이다. 이런 사람들이 텔레비전을 볼 때 광고가
그들의 머릿속에 쉽게 주입되기 때문이다. 데렌은 자신의 쇼를
성공시키는 방법을 알고 자신이 다루기 쉬운 방청객을 찾을 수
도 있다. 데렌은 자신의 몇몇 쇼에서 한두 마디의 말만으로 사
람에게 최면을 거는 것이 얼마나 쉬운지 보여 준다.

데렌은 전통적 마술 기법, 기억의 기술, 최면술, 몸짓 읽기, 인
지 심리학을 포함한 다양한 방법을 이용해 환영을 만들어 낸다.
데렌은 자신의 지식과 기술을 사용해서 사람들의 생각을 예측
하고 영향을 미칠 뿐 아니라 사람들의 생각을 나타내는 미묘한
신체적 신호를 읽는 능력이 있는 것으로 보인다.

일부 사람들은 데렌이 쇼에서 배우나 조연을 사용한다고 말하
며 그의 능력을 의심한다. 하지만, 데렌은 자신의 일에 그런 사
람들을 절대 쓰지 않는다고 주장한다. 당신은 그가 그런 환상
적인 재능이 있다는 사실을 믿을 수 있는가?

◯ 해설

1 이 글의 주요 내용은 무엇인가?
  a. 데렌 브라운과 그의 속임수
  b. 무대 최면술사의 위력
  c. 데렌 브라운과 그의 능력
  d. 최면술과 인지 심리학
  e. 평범한 사람들을 조종하는 방법

2 "predict"의 뜻에 가장 가까운 단어는 무엇인가?
  a. 성취하다
  b. 무시하다
  c. 예측하다
  d. 분명히 하다
  e. 경고하다

3 빈칸에 들어갈 가장 적절한 단어는 무엇인가?
  a. 속이다
  b. 가리키다
  c. 가까스로 해내다
  d. 가르치다
  e. 대우하다

4 이 글에서 유추할 수 있는 내용은 무엇인가?
  a. 대부분의 사람들은 쉽게 최면에 걸릴 수 없다.
  b. 데렌은 곧 쇼에서 은퇴할 것이다.
  c. 거의 모든 사람이 최면에 걸릴 수 있을 것이다.
  d. 사람들은 텔레비전을 보면서 최면에 걸리는 것을 좋아한다.
  e. 일부 사람들은 다른 사람들보다 쉽게 최면에 걸린다.

5 "them"이 가리키는 것은 무엇인가?

◯ 구문해설

3행_ This means that he did a show where he picked out
    audience members, brought them up on the stage, and
    hypnotized them to do strange things.
⇨ 접속사 that이 명사절을 이끌어 동사 means의 목적어 역할을 하고 있다.
  picked out, brought, hypnotized는 주어 he와 연결되어 병렬관계를 이
  루고 있다.

6행_ The person will then enter sort of a trance and do
    whatever Derren says.
⇨ whatever는 복합 관계대명사로 명사절을 이끌어 동사 do의 목적어 역할을 하
  고 있다.

8행_ the adult will suddenly start talking like he/she did
    when he/she was five and begin running around the
    room playing with everything
⇨ like는 접속사로 '~와 똑같이, ~처럼'이라는 의미이다. playing with every-
  thing는 분사구문으로 의미상의 주어는 the adult이다.

15행_ Derren demonstrates how easy it is to hypnotize
                          가주어   진주어
    people with just a word or two.
⇨ demonstrates와 how 사이에 접속사 that이 생략되었다.

UNIT 7-1 Viral Art

◯ Pre-reading Activity

1. ⓓ   2. ⓐ   3. ⓑ   4. ⓒ

◯ 정답

1. c   2. b   3. c   4. d   5. c

◯ 해석

예술은, 종이에 온통 케첩을 뿌리는 18개월 된 유아부터 레오
나르도 다 빈치와 미켈란젤로와 같은 거장에 이르기까지 어디
에나 존재한다. 최근 영국 출신의 한 신인 예술가가 유리 예술
로 화제를 일으키고 있다. 이 유리 예술은 아름다울지는 모르
지만 약간의 치명적인 왜곡이 있다.

그 조각가인 루크 제람은 HIV, 천연두, 그리고 돼지 독감 바이
러스로 더 흔히 알려진 최근의 신종 플루와 같은 치명적인 바이
러스에 대해 공부하는 데 몇 년을 쏟았다. 그는 이 작은 치명적

인 것들을 5년 이상 연구해서 이를 유리로 표현했다. 이런 새로운 예술 형식에 대한 반응은 놀라웠다. 그 고약한 바이러스들은 우윳빛 유리에 아름답게 표현되어 거울로 된 표면 위에서 크리스털처럼 빛을 낸다. 이 투명하고 깨질 것만 같은 구체(球體)들은 실제로 인류 역사상 가장 치명적인 것들이었다.

제람은 텔레비전과 여러 잡지 기사에서 이 치명적인 바이러스를 주제로 하는 실례(實例)를 보고 나서 바이러스에 관심을 갖게 되었다. 그가 관심을 갖게 된 경로는 흥미롭다. 그는 바이러스가 너무 작아서 전자 현미경으로도 세밀히 볼 수 없다는 것을 알게 되었다. 그는 이런 바이러스를 백만 배 더 크게 만들면 사람들이 그것들을 더 잘 이해하거나 최소한 더 쉽게 식별할 수 있으리라 생각했다.

제람은 사람들이 이 작은 생물을 보고 이들이 인류에게 미치는 영향을 더 잘 이해하기를 원했다. 그토록 작은 것들이 매년 그렇게 많은 사람을 죽일 수 있다는 것은 정말 깜짝 놀랄 일이다. 제람은 우리가 그 점에 대해 생각해 보기를 원한다. 제람은 연구를 진행하는 동안, 바이러스학자조차도 바이러스의 여러 측면과 그것이 작용하는 방식을 완전히 이해하지 못한다는 사실을 알게 되었다. 그는 우리가 이 많은 의문에 대한 해결책을 찾을 수 있기를 바란다. 그는 자신의 예술 작품이 사람들이 바이러스라는 적에 대해 더 많이 알게 되는 데 도움이 되기를 바란다. 더욱 중요하게는 이 치명적인 병균에 대항할 치료법을 발견할지도 모르는 미래의 과학자들에게 영감을 주기를 희망한다.

◎ 해설

1 이 글의 주요 내용은 무엇인가?
　a. 바이러스 예술의 감상
　b. 치명적인 바이러스의 극심한 영향력
　c. 바이러스를 이용한 새로운 예술 유형의 창조
　d. 루크 제람과 그의 놀라운 삶
　e. 창의적인 화가와 영감을 주는 그의 예술 작품

2 글쓴이가 "Art is everywhere"를 언급한 이유는 무엇인가?
　a. 예술이 어렵다는 것을 설명하려고
　b. 무엇이든 예술 작품이 될 수 있다고 말하려고
　c. 예술가를 사방에서 발견할 수 있다고 말하려고
　d. 예술은 이해하기 힘들다고 설명하려고
　e. 예술 작품은 어디에나 설치될 수 있다고 주장하려고

3 "appreciate"의 뜻에 가장 가까운 단어는 무엇인가?
　a. 만족시키다
　b. 경시하다
　c. 이해하다
　d. 달성하다
　e. 할당하다

4 빈칸에 들어갈 가장 적절한 단어는 무엇인가?
　　　(A)　　　　(B)
　a. 작은　　　　처방하다
　b. 커다란　　　비판하다
　c. 충분한　　　추정하다
　d. 작은　　　　이해하다
　e. 아주 작은　　진단하다

5 루크 제람에 대한 설명 중 사실이 아닌 것은 무엇인가?
　a. 그는 유리를 이용해서 바이러스의 모양을 확대한다.
　b. 그는 사람들이 이 치명적인 바이러스를 이해하기를 원한다.
　c. 그의 새로운 예술 유형은 사람들에게 과소평가되었다.
　d. 그는 미래에 과학자들이 치명적인 바이러스의 치료법을 발견하기를 원한다.
　e. 그는 사람들이 바이러스가 인간에 미치는 영향력을 알아야 한다고 생각한다.

◎ 구문해설

7행_ This glass art, beautiful <u>as</u> it may be, has a bit of a deadly twist to it.
⇒ as는 접속사로 양보를 나타내어 '~이기는 하지만'이라는 의미이다.
☆ Young as she is, she can speak English very well.
　(그녀는 어리지만 영어를 매우 잘한다.)

12행_ he has studied these tiny killers and is now <u>having them blown</u> in glass
⇒ having them blown은 「사역동사＋목적어＋과거분사(목적격 보어)」의 구조이며 목적어와 목적격 보어가 수동의 관계이다.

14행_ Beautifully <u>rendered in milky glass</u>, the nasty viruses shimmer like crystal on mirrored surfaces.
⇒ Beautifully rendered in milky glass는 수동 분사구문으로 의미상의 주어는 the nasty viruses이다.

19행_ He learned viruses are <u>so</u> small <u>that</u> even electron microscopes cannot make out all of their details.
⇒ 「so ~ that …」은 '대단히 ~해서 …하다'의 뜻으로 that은 생략될 수 있다.

22행_ Jerram <u>wants</u> <u>people</u> <u>to see</u> these little critters and better <u>understand</u> the impact <u>they</u> have on humanity.
⇒ 「want＋목적어＋to부정사」의 문장 구조를 알아두자. 동사 understand 앞에 to가 생략되었으며, the impact와 they 사이에 목적격 관계대명사가 생략되었다.

23행_ <u>For</u> something so small <u>to kill</u> so many people each year is truly mind-boggling.
⇒ 전치사 For는 to부정사의 의미상의 주어로 「for＋목적어＋to부정사」는 '~이 … 하는 것'라는 의미이다.
☆ <u>For</u> me <u>to live</u> with him was torture. (그와 함께 산다는 것은 고문이었다.)

28행_ he hopes to inspire future scientists who may be the ones to find cures to these deadly bugs

⇒ the ones는 부정대명사로 scientists를 의미한다. to find는 to부정사의 형용사적 용법으로 쓰여 the ones를 수식하고 있다.

UNIT 7-2 Art Collage

○ Pre-reading Activity

stones, stuck, glue

○ 정답

1. c 2. c 3. d 4. a 5. one's creativity

○ 해석

학교에서 미술 수업을 받아본 적이 있는 사람이면 누구나 분명히 콜라주 미술에 친숙할 것이다. 콜라주는 재미있게 작품을 만들 수 있을 뿐만 아니라 누구든지 할 수 있어서 전 세계 학생들에게 가장 인기 있는 예술 활동 중 하나이다. 좋든 싫든 간에 콜라주로 알려진 예술 유형이 다시 유행하고 있다. 이 유행은 공립학교와 사립학교에 다니는 유치원생부터 12학년에 이르는 학생들 사이에만 일어나는 것이 아니다. 성인 학습 센터는 젊은이부터 오늘날을 살아가는 일부 노인에 이르기까지 모든 사람에게 이 창의적인 수업을 제공하고 있다.

흥미진진한 콜라주 작품을 만들기 위해 필요한 것은 다양한 재료와 풀, 종이나 나무 판, 또는 캔버스 같은 바탕이 전부이다. 재료는 신문과 잡지에서 잘라낸 것부터 사진, 천 조각, 밧줄, 끈에 이르기까지 어떤 것이든 될 수 있다. 사람의 창의성만이 어떤 종류의 재료가 콜라주에 쓰일 수 있는지에 대한 유일한 제한이 된다.

일단 이 모든 재료를 갖추고 나면 콜라주를 조합해 만들거나 구성하기 시작할 수 있다. 한 가지 방법은 아무것도 없는 바탕 위에 모든 재료를 풀로 붙여서 진정한 자신만의 그림이나 디자인을 만드는 것이다. 오래 가는 걸작을 만들기 위해서는 적절한 접착제를 사용하는 것이 매우 중요하다. 품질이 좋지 않은 접착제를 사용하면 오래 가지 않아 거실 바닥에 떨어진 콜라주를 발견할 것이다!

콜라주를 만드는 또 다른 방법은 자신이 이미 만든 그림이나 소묘 위에 재료를 붙이는 것이다. 이런 방법으로 자신의 재료를 사용해 3차원 효과를 내거나 질감을 더해 그림을 완성할 수 있다. 무엇을 만들지는 전적으로 자신과 자신의 상상력에 달려 있으므로 어떤 방법을 선택하든 콜라주는 재미있다.

○ 해설

1 첫 번째 문단의 주요 내용은 무엇인가?
   a. 콜라주 미술과 그것의 창의적 과정
   b. 콜라주를 만들 때 필요한 재료들
   c. 콜라주로 알려진 미술 유형의 부활
   d. 훌륭한 콜라주 미술 만들기 위해 자신의 상상력을 이용하기
   e. 다양한 재료로 콜라주 미술 조합하는 방법

2 "inferior"의 뜻에 가장 가까운 단어는 무엇인가?
   a. 우수한
   b. 값비싼
   c. 표준 이하의
   d. 상세한
   e. 전형적인

3 다음 중 사실이 아닌 것은 무엇인가?
   a. 훌륭한 콜라주 미술 작품에는 적절한 접착제가 필요하다.
   b. 콜라주에 자신이 좋아하는 어떤 재료라도 쓸 수 있다.
   c. 아무것도 없는 표면에 재료를 붙여서 콜라주를 만들기 시작할 수 있다.
   d. 대부분의 사람들은 콜라주라는 예술 유형에 친숙하지 않다.
   e. 오늘날 모든 연령층의 사람들이 콜라주 미술 작품을 만들 기회가 있다.

4 빈칸에 들어갈 가장 적절한 단어는 무엇인가?

> 콜라주는 신문, 사진, 옷감, 끈 등의 다양한 재료를 조합해서 만든 시각 미술이다. 비어 있는 표면 위에 자신이 원하는 재료를 자신만의 아이디어로 구성해 작품이 달라질 수 있다.

   a. 재료, 아이디어
   b. 붓, 직원
   c. 내용, 옷
   d. 연결, 독립
   e. 특징, 그림

5 글쓴이는 콜라주에 쓰일 수 있는 것들을 제한하는 것이 무엇이라 말하는가?

○ 구문해설

13행_ To make an exciting collage, all you need is a bunch of different materials, some glue, and a surface such as pieces of paper, wood panels, or canvases.

⇒ To make an exciting collage는 to부정사의 부사적 용법 중 목적을 나타낸다. all과 you 사이에 관계대명사 that이 생략되었으며, all은 단수 취급하여 동사 is가 왔다는 것에 주의하자.

19행_ One method is to paste all of your materials onto a plain surface to create pictures or designs that are truly your own.

⇒ to paste ~ your own은 to부정사구로 주격 보어 역할을 한다. that은 주격 관계대명사로 선행사는 pictures or designs이다.

23행_ Another approach to making a collage is to glue your materials onto a painting or <u>drawing you</u> have already created.

⇨ drawing과 you 사이에 목적격 관계대명사가 생략되었다.

24행_ In this way, you can use your materials to complete your picture <u>giving it a three-dimensional effect or an added texture</u>.

⇨ giving it a three-dimensional effect or an added texture는 분사구문으로 의미상의 주어는 you이다.

26행_ <u>Whichever</u> way you choose, collages are fun because <u>whatever</u> you decide to make is entirely up to you and your own imagination!

⇨ Whichever는 복합 관계형용사이고, whatever는 복합 관계대명사로 명사절을 이끌어 주어 역할을 하고 있다.

UNIT 8-1 Snakes: A Good Story

Pre-reading Activity

1. T   2. F   3. F

정답

1. d   2. e   3. e   4. c   5. It squeezes Daniel.

해석

다니엘 그린은 간질 환자다. 간질은 경련이나 발작을 일으키는 두뇌 질환이다. 간질을 앓는 사람이 발작이 일어나리라는 것을 미리 알면 안전한 장소로 가서 앉을 수 있다. 이는 번화한 거리에서 발작이 일어나면 위험할 수 있기 때문에 아주 중요하다.

이 장애를 지닌 소수의 사람들은 발작 경고견을 데리고 있다. 발작 경고견을 훈련시키는 데는 2년이나 걸려 발작 경고견을 소유할 수 있는 사람들은 많지 않다. 일부 사람들은 발작 경고견을 소유하기 위해 10년을 기다리기도 한다. 특별하게 훈련받은 개는 사람의 신체에 일어나는 변화를 느껴서 발작이 일어날 거라고 주인에게 알릴 수 있다. 그러면 그 사람은 안전한 장소로 갈 수 있다.

다니엘 그린은 발작 경고견을 얻기 위해 기다리고 싶지 않았다. 그는 자신의 애완동물인 거의 5피트의 길이에 달하는 보아 뱀이 (발작 경고견이 하는 일과) 똑같은 일을 할 수 있다는 사실을 알고 있었다. 그는 자신이 발작을 일으키리라는 사실을 보아 뱀이 어떻게 알 수 있는지는 설명할 수 없었다. 어느 날, 다니엘

이 자신의 애완동물인 보아 뱀을 목에 두르고 TV를 보며 앉아 있을 때 발작이 일어나기 몇 분 전에 보아 뱀이 다니엘을 꽉 휘감았다. 그런 일이 있고 나서 다니엘은 어디를 가든 그 뱀을 데리고 다녔다. 그는 은행, 우체국, 식료품 가게를 비롯해서 어디든지 보아 뱀을 데려갔다.

다니엘이 어떤 장소에 가든 그곳 관리자나 직원들이 다니엘에게 "이곳에 그 뱀을 데려오면 안 됩니다! 당장 나가세요!"라고 소리쳤다. 다니엘은 공공장소에서 많은 사람들이 자신의 애완동물을 보고 불쾌해한다는 사실을 알았다.

다니엘과 그의 변호사는 보아 뱀도 발작 경고견과 같은 임무를 수행할 수 있다는 사실을 증명했다. 그 결과, 그의 보아 뱀은 그가 가는 곳이라면 어디든지 함께 갈 수 있다. 보아 뱀을 목에 감고 자동차를 운전해 가는 사람을 본다면 그 사람은 아마도 다니엘과 그의 애완동물인 보아 뱀 "레드록"일 것이다.

해설

1 이 글의 주요 내용은 무엇인가?
   a. 전 세계적인 발작 경고견의 증가
   b. 간질병 환자를 위해 특별하게 훈련 받은 뱀
   c. 간질이라는 질병과 일상생활에서 그것이 작용하는 방식
   d. 다니엘 그린과 그의 발작 경고 뱀에 얽힌 놀라운 이야기
   e. 장애인과 발작 경고 동물의 관계

2 "forthcoming"의 뜻에 가장 가까운 단어는 무엇인가?
   a. 사라진
   b. 먼
   c. 필연적인
   d. 피할 수 있는
   e. 다가오는

3 이 글에서 유추할 수 있는 내용은 무엇인가?
   a. 다니엘은 뱀을 공공장소에 데려가려고 훈련시켰다.
   b. 사람들은 발작 경고 동물을 키우는 것이 매우 멋진 일이라 생각한다.
   c. 사람들은 어떤 종류의 보조 동물이라도 가까이 있는 것을 좋아하지 않는다.
   d. 간질을 앓는 사람은 발작 경고견을 쉽게 구할 수 있다.
   e. 사람들은 발작 경고 동물로 뱀보다는 개를 더욱 편안해 할지도 모른다.

4 다음 문장이 들어갈 가장 적절한 곳은 어디인가?

> 그러나 자신의 애완동물을 공공장소에 데려가는 데는 한 가지 문제가 있었다.

5 보아 뱀은 다니엘에게 발작이 일어나리라는 사실을 어떻게 경고하는가?

구문해설

1행_ Epilepsy is a disorder of the brain <u>that</u> results in convulsions or seizures.

⇨ that은 주격 관계대명사로 선행사는 a disorder이다.

13행_ When Daniel was sitting around <u>watching TV with his pet python wrapped around his neck</u> one day,

⇨ watching TV with his pet python wrapped around his neck은 분사구문으로 의미상의 주어는 Daniel이다.

⇨ 「with+명사+분사」는 분사구문의 형태로 '~을 …한 채로'라는 의미로 쓰인다. 분사가 현재분사일 경우에는 명사와의 관계가 능동이고, 과거분사일 경우에는 수동이다.

☆ I used to take a walk in the morning <u>with my dog following me</u>. (능동: 나는 나를 따라오는 개를 데리고 아침에 산책하고 했다.)

☆ She fell asleep <u>with the light turned on</u>.
(수동: 그녀는 불을 켜둔 채 잠들었다.)

19행_ He noticed <u>that</u> many people in public were uncomfortable when they saw his pet.

⇨ that은 접속사로 동사 noticed의 목적어 역할을 하는 명사절을 이끈다.

25행_ If you ever <u>see</u> a man <u>driving</u> down the road with a python around his neck, that is probably Daniel and his pet python "Redrock."

⇨ If는 가정이 아닌 조건절을 이끌며, 지각동사 see의 목적격 보어로 현재분사(driving)가 왔다.

UNIT 8-2 The Sanctuary

● 정답

1. b 2. c 3. b 4. c 5. other animal-rights advocates in the area

---

● 해석

안타깝게도 콜롬비아는 눈부시게 아름다운 자연과 놀랍도록 다양한 생물로 유명하기보다는 마약 거래로 더 유명하다. 하지만, 칼리 시에서 들려오는 긍정적인 이야기도 있다. 이는 아나 줄리아 토레스의 이야기이다. 토레스는 작은 학교의 교장이자 구조된 다양한 동물을 위한 보호소를 운영하게 된 동물 권리 보호 옹호자이기도 하다.

800마리가 넘는 동물을 수용하고 있는 토레스가 운영하는 보호소에는 아이러니하게도 마약 사업과 연관되어 있다. 그녀가 수용해서 돌보는 동물의 대부분은 그 지역의 많은 마약 거래상들의 소유였다. 마약계의 거물 몇몇이 체포되거나 살해당하면 커다란 아프리카 사자부터 피그미마모셋에 이르는 많은 동물들이 남겨진다. 그러면 경찰은 가장 먼저 토레스에게 연락해서 동물을 데려가 달라고 요청한다.

토레스가 운영하는 보호소는 동물을 밀수하려다 체포된 사람들로부터 동물을 넘겨받기도 한다. 이는 콜롬비아에 서식하는 생물이 매우 다양해 동물들을 몰래 나라 안팎으로 빼돌려서 돈벌이를 하는 사람이 많기 때문이다. 붙잡힌 동물에는 오색 콘도르, 큰부리새, 거미원숭이, 카이만(중남미산 악어)이 있고 심지어 퓨마도 있다. 이들 동물은 모두 남은 삶을 보호소에서 지내게 된다. 이익을 위해 자신들을 이용하려는 인간에 대해 걱정할 필요가 없는 것이다.

토레스는 칼리 환경 경찰과 개인 기부자의 지원만을 받을 뿐 콜롬비아 정부의 기금은 받지 않는다. 해당 지역에는 토레스가 운영하는 보호소의 성장을 우려하는 다른 동물 권리 옹호자들이 있기는 하지만, 그들은 여전히 토레스의 보호소를 지지한다. 언젠가 콜롬비아가 현재의 악명에서 벗어나 야생생물과 동물의 안식처로 유명해지기를 바란다.

● 해설

1 이 글의 주요 내용은 무엇인가?
a. 콜롬비아의 다양한 생물과 아름다움
b. 아나 줄리아 토레스가 운영하는 동물 보호소
c. 콜롬비아 마약 사업의 부작용
d. 사람들이 콜롬비아 밖으로 밀수출하려는 동물들
e. 동물 보호소에 무관심한 태도를 보이는 콜롬비아 정부

2 "lucrative"의 뜻에 가장 가까운 단어는 무엇인가?
a. 적절한
b. 무익한
c. 이익이 되는
d. 적당한
e. 비생산적인

3 빈칸에 들어갈 가장 적절한 단어는 무엇인가?
a. 대신에
b. 바라건대
c. 그러므로
d. 진심으로
e. 불행하게도

4 다음 중 사실이 아닌 것은 무엇인가?
a. 콜롬비아 사람들은 돈을 벌기 위해 동물을 밀수한다.
b. 토레스는 구조된 동물들을 죽을 때까지 보호한다.
c. 토레스는 자신의 학교를 구조된 동물을 수용하는 보호소로 사용한다.
d. 토레스의 보호소에서는 여러 종류의 동물을 많이 볼 수 있다.
e. 토레스의 보호소는 동물이 보살핌을 받을 수 있는 곳이다.

5 "they"가 가리키는 것은 무엇인가?

● 구문해설

7행_ Most of the animals <u>that</u> she takes in and cares for <u>come</u> from many of the local drug traffickers.

⇨ 관계대명사 that이 형용사절을 이끌어 주어 Most of the animals를 수식하고 있으며, 본동사는 come이다.

10행_ One of the first calls that the police make is to Torres to request that she take in the animals.

⇨ 접속사 that은 request의 목적어 역할을 하는 명사절을 이끌고 있다. 요구를 나타내는 동사 request로 인해 take 앞에는 조동사 should가 생략되었다. 「요구·제안·주장을 나타내는 동사+that+주어+(should)+동사원형」의 문장 구조를 알아두자.

☆ I insisted that he attend the annual meeting.
(나는 그가 연례회의에 참여해야 한다고 주장했다.)

12행_ Torres' sanctuary also gets other critters coming from people who are caught trying to smuggle animals.

⇨ coming은 현재분사로 other critters를 후치 수식하고 있다. who는 주격 관계대명사로 선행사는 people이다. trying to smuggle animals는 분사 구문으로 의미상의 주어는 people이다.

17행_ They do not have to worry about humans trying to exploit them for profit.

⇨ trying은 현재분사로 humans를 후치 수식하고 있다.

UNIT 9-1　What about Becoming a Zoologist?

○ **Pre-reading Activity**

aspects, habitats, zoos

○ **정답**

1. b　2. e　3. b　4. b　5. d

○ **해석**

동물학자는 연구실과 자연 서식지에서 동물이 사는 방식과 환경에 적응하는 방식을 연구하는 과학자다. 동물학자는 동물을 면밀히 연구해 동물을 분류하고, 동물이 개별적으로 또는 집단과 사회의 구성원으로 어떤 역할을 하는지 이해할 수 있다. 그들은 파충류와 양서류 같은 생물을 연구하기도 한다. 그들은 때때로 동물을 포획해서 진정시킨 후 수의사에게 데려가 동물의 건강 상태를 점검한다. 그런 후에는 동물을 야생으로 돌려보낸다.

동물학자는 캐나다 늑대가 멸종 위기에 처해 있다는 말을 들었을 것이다. 이 말이 사실인지, 늑대의 멸종 위기가 얼마나 급박한지 파악하기 위해서는 현장 조사를 해야 한다. 동물학자는 늑대가 서식하는 지역이 어디인지, 어디서 어떻게 자는지, 한

무리에 몇 마리의 늑대가 있는지, 늑대의 먹이가 무엇인지 알고 있다. 이런 정보를 갖춘 동물학자는 소지품을 챙겨서 멸종 위기에 처한 늑대가 사는 구역으로 들어간다. 동물학자는 늑대의 굴을 발견해서 늑대가 몇 마리나 서식하고 있는지 파악한다. 동물학자는 늑대가 생활하는 주변 환경에 음식이 충분한지 확인하기 위해 늑대의 서식지를 점검한다. 그 다음에는 해당 지역에 늑대들의 생존을 위협하는 건설 행위나 기타 파괴 행위가 있는지 살펴본다.

동물학자는 현장 조사를 끝낸 후에 사무실로 돌아와 늑대의 현황에 대해 장문의 보고서와 권고사항을 쓴다. 이는 쉬운 일이 아니다. 동물학자가 늑대를 발견하고, 늑대와 마주칠 때 자신을 보호하려면 늑대의 서식지와 본성을 충분히 연구해야 한다. 또한 동물학자들은 자연사 박물관, 동물원, 연구실, 국립공원에서도 일한다. 다수는 대학에서 가르치거나 환경 컨설턴트로 일한다. 동물학자가 되고 싶다면 정보를 통합하는 작업을 즐겨야 한다. 또한 인내심을 갖추고 매우 체계적이어야 하며 방심해서는 안 된다. 이는 동물학자가 연구를 계속 수행하고, 엄청난 양의 정보를 다루고, 예측할 수 없는 동물 행동에 노출될 수밖에 없는 일을 하기 때문이다.

○ **해설**

1 이 글의 주요 내용은 무엇인가?
  a. 동물학자가 될 때 따르는 위험
  b. 동물학자에 대한 전반적 직무 서술
  c. 동물학자가 캐나다 늑대를 연구하는 방법
  d. 동물학자가 연구해야 하는 여러 동물
  e. 동물학자가 갖추어야 할 학력

2 "tranquilize"의 뜻에 가장 가까운 단어는 무엇인가?
  a. 의지하다
  b. 제출하다
  c. 완전히 없애다
  d. 깨끗이 치우다
  e. 진정시키다

3 밑줄 친 "they"가 가리키는 명사가 다른 것을 고르시오.

4 빈칸에 들어갈 가장 적절한 말은 무엇인가?
  a. 수의사가 필요하다면
  b. 우연히 마주친다면
  c. 늑대가 더 자주 새끼를 낳는다면
  d. 늑대가 완전히 멸종된다면
  e. 늑대가 낯선 사람을 무서워한다면

5 이 글에서 유추할 수 있는 내용은 무엇인가?
  a. 동물학자는 항상 현장에서 일한다.
  b. 동물학자는 주로 파충류 연구에 주력한다.
  c. 동물학자는 야생에서 현장 조사를 수행하지 않는다.

d. 동물학자는 멸종 위기에 처한 동물을 주의 깊게 관찰한다.

e. 동물학자는 동물 행동의 모든 측면을 예측할 수 있다.

● 구문해설

11행_ Armed with this information, the zoologist will pack up his/her belongings and go into the territories where these endangered wolves live.

⇒ Armed with this information은 분사구문으로 의미상의 주어는 the zoologist다. where는 관계부사로 선행사는 the territories이다.

14행_ The zoologist will check their habitats to make sure there is enough food in their surroundings.

⇒ make sure와 there 사이에 명사절을 이끄는 접속사 that이 생략되었다.

15행_ Then, the zoologist will check if there is any construction or other destruction in the area that would threaten the wolves.

⇒ 접속사 if는 '~인지, 아닌지'라는 의미로 명사절을 이끌어 동사 check의 목적어 역할을 한다. that은 주격 관계대명사로 선행사는 any construction or other destruction이다.

25행_ You also need to be patient, well organized, and alert since the work involves keeping track of research, handling huge amounts of data, and being exposed to unpredictable animal behavior.

⇒ to be 이하 patient, well organized, alert가 병렬관계를 이루고 있다. keeping, handling, being exposed 역시 동사 involves와 연결되어 병렬관계를 이루고 있다. 접속사 since는 '~이므로, ~이기 때문에'라는 의미로 이유를 나타낸다.

UNIT 9-2 Predicting the Future & Future Jobs

● 정답

1. e 2. a 3. a 4. d 5. because of space tourism in its infancy

● 해석

미래는 예측이 불가능하지만, 미래학자들이 미래가 어떠할지 예측하기 위해 최선을 다하는 것을 막을 수는 없다. 지난 100여 년간 미래를 예측하는 데 어려움을 겪었던 사람들의 말을 살펴보자.

1977년에 디지털 장비회사의 회장인 켄 올슨은 "사람들이 자기 집에 컴퓨터를 가지고 있을 이유가 전혀 없다."라고 말했다.

좀 더 과거로 거슬러 올라가서, 미시건 저축 은행의 은행장은 포드 자동차사에 투자하는 문제를 놓고 헨리 포드의 변호사와 대화를 나누는 중에 "말은 널리 보급될 것이지만, 자동차는 진기한 상품으로 일시적 유행일 뿐입니다."라고 말했다. 또 다른 이야기가 있다. 1878년에 영국 체신공사 사장은 "미국인에게는 전화가 필요하지만 우리는 전화가 필요 없습니다. 우리에게는 메신저 보이가 많이 있습니다."라고 말했다.

보다시피 완벽한 사람은 아무도 없다. 우리가 내리는 예측은 때때로 어긋난다. 앞서 예로 든 사람들의 말이 맞았다면 수백 만 명에 이르는 컴퓨터 프로그래머, 공학자, 설계자, 조작자, 전기 기술자 등의 직업은 생겨나지 않았을 것이다. 그렇다면 일부 과학 및 기술 관련 직업의 미래는 어떨까? '퓨처 사비'에 근무하는 사람들은 미래가 어떤 모습일지, 어떤 종류의 직업이 필요한지 정확하게 예측하기 위해 열심히 일하고 있다.

2020~2030년에 창출될 그들이 예측한 몇 가지 흥미로운 직업은 다음과 같다.

• 신체 부위 제작자: 장기와 팔다리 같은 인체 부위를 만들 것이다. 신체 부위를 만드는 제작자, 상점, 심지어는 수리점까지 필요할 것이다.

• 우주 조종사, 우주 건축가, 우주여행 안내자: 현재 우주 관광업은 초기 단계에 있으므로 틀림없이 발전할 것이고, 우주 조종사, 우주 건축가, 우주여행 안내자가 필요할 것은 분명하다.

미래의 직업을 소개하는 몇몇 링크를 탐색해보고 어떤 직업이 흥미로울지 살펴보자!

● 해설

1 두 번째 문단의 주요 내용은 무엇인가?

a. 미래학자와 그들의 예측

b. 미래와 미래에 대한 예측 불가능성

c. 몇몇 미래의 흥미로운 직업

d. 우주 관광업과 그것의 불확실한 미래

e. 사람들이 언급했던 부정확한 예측의 실례

2 빈칸에 들어갈 가장 적절한 말은 무엇인가?

a. 완벽한 사람은 아무도 없다.

b. 서두르면 일을 그르친다.

c. 우리에게는 점쟁이가 필요하다.

d. 사람들은 자신의 운명을 믿지 않는다.

e. 영국인은 전화를 가지고 있지 않다.

3 "quoted"의 뜻에 가장 가까운 단어는 무엇인가?

a. 인용하다

b. 분류하다

c. 분리하다

d. 부제를 달다

e. 비평하다

4 다음 중 사실이 아닌 것은 무엇인가?

  a. 미래학자의 일은 미래를 예측하는 것이다.

  b. 미래에 일어날 일을 예측하기는 쉽지 않다.

  c. 미래에는 더 많은 사람들이 우주여행을 할 것이다.

  d. 전화는 1870년대 후반에 널리 보급되었다.

  e. 본문에서 인용한 사람들의 예측은 모두 빗나갔다.

5 글쓴이가 우주 비행사가 미래의 직업이 될 수 있다고 언급한 이유는 무엇인가?

___

◐ 구문해설

1행_ The future is unpredictable, but that does not stop futurists from doing the best they can to figure out what the future will look like.

⇨ that은 대명사로 앞의 내용인 The future is unpredictable을 의미한다. what the future will look like는 명사절로 figure out의 목적어 역할을 하고 있다. to figure out는 to부정사의 부사적 용법 중 목적을 나타낸다.

6행_ the president of the Michigan Savings Bank, while talking to Henry Ford's lawyer about investing in Ford Motor Company, said, "*The horse is here to stay, but the automobile is only a novelty, a fad.*"

⇨ while talking to Henry Ford's lawyer about investing in Ford Motor Company는 분사구문으로 의미상의 주어는 the president이다. 접속사 while은 '~하는 동안'이라는 의미이다.

12행_ If the gentlemen quoted above had been correct, we would not have had millions of computer programmers, engineers, designers, operators, electricians, just to name a few.

⇨ 가정법 과거완료의 형태는 「if+주어+had +과거분사~, 주어+조동사(would, could)+have+과거분사」이다. 과거분사 quoted는 주어 the gentlemen을 후치 수식하고 있다.

UNIT 10-1   Rites of Passage

◐ Pre-reading Activity

Aborigines, New Zealand

◐ 정답

1. e   2. c   3. a   4. b   5. **They go on a personal, spiritual quest alone in the wilderness.**

◐ 해석

10대와 젊은 청년들은 아이에서 성인이 되었음을 증명하기 위해 역사적으로 통과 의례를 치러야 했다. 일반적으로 통과 의례는 아이들이 자신이 속한 집단에서 성인으로 인정받기 위해 성공적으로 수행해야 하는 어려운 임무를 가리킨다.

오스트레일리아의 원주민 소년들이 한 번 가는 데 몇 주가 걸리는 험악한 오스트레일리아 오지로의 긴 도보여행을 가야 한다는 사실을 알고 있는 사람은 많다. 그들은 이런 임무를 혼자 수행하고, 호된 시련을 이기고 살아남아 집으로 돌아와야 했다. 소년이 돌아오면 부족에서는 그가 이제 성인이 되었다고 축하해 준다.

일부 아메리카 원주민 부족은 좀 더 나이가 많은 아이들에게 사람이 살지 않는 산악 지역인 황무지에서 홀로 개인적이고 영적인 탐구를 수행하라고 명한다. 이 통과 의례에는 일반적으로 금식과 명상이 포함된다. 그들은 여러 날 동안 자신의 영혼이 다시 태어날 수 있는 경지에 이르기 위해 길잡이를 찾는다. 그러고 나서 그들은 집으로 돌아와 부족 내에서의 자신의 역할과 삶의 목표를 말한다.

정통 유대교 신앙에서 남녀 아이들은 성경을 공부하고 방대한 양의 성구를 외워야 한다. 젊은이들은 자신이 종교적으로 사회의 일원이 될 준비를 갖췄다는 사실을 보여 주기 위해 가족과 친구가 모인 자리에서 성경 구절을 암송해야 한다. 그러면 소년에게는 바르미츠바, 소녀에게는 바트미츠바라는 성대한 파티를 보상으로 열어 준다. 축하 파티에서는 그들의 성취와 통과 의례를 축하하기 위해 멋진 선물과 음식을 제공한다.

현대 사회에도 여전히 이런 고대 관습의 일부가 존재하지만, 전 세계 많은 젊은이들은 더 이상 성인으로의 통과를 나타내는 어떤 행사에도 참여하지 않는다. 통과 의례가 필요한가? 10대로서 자신이 더 이상 아이가 아니라는 사실을 증명하는 어떤 혹독한 행동을 수행해 보고 싶은가? 그에 대한 답례로 성인으로 대우받고 성인으로서의 책임을 맡게 될 것이라 생각하는가?

___

◐ 해설

1 이 글의 주요 내용은 무엇인가?

  a. 젊은이에서 성인으로의 변화

  b. 현대 사회에서 젊은이들을 위한 새로운 관행

  c. 오래 전에 오스트레일리아에 도착한 원주민

  d. 아이들의 성장을 축하할 필요성

  e. 전통적인 통과 의례와 그것들의 소멸

2 "rigorous"의 뜻에 가장 가까운 단어는 무엇인가?

  a. 정확한

  b. 경건한

  c. 엄한

  d. 애매한

  e. 관대한

3 다음 중 사실이 아닌 것은 무엇인가?

a. 많은 전통적 통과 의례가 여전히 치러지고 있다.

b. 미국 원주민 소년들은 정신적 탐구를 진행하는 동안 금식한다.

c. 정통 유대교 아이들은 통과 의례로 성경 구절을 암송한다.

d. 대부분의 통과 의례에는 아이들이 수행하기에 다소 어려운 임무가 포함된다.

e. 오스트레일리아 원주민 소년들은 통과 의례로 몇 주간 도보여행을 해야 했다.

4 빈칸에 들어갈 적절한 단어는 무엇인가?

> 통과 의례는 어떤 사람이 청년에서 성인이 되었음을 나타내는 의식이다. 각 문화에는 고유의 통과 의례가 있지만 오늘날에는 쇠퇴하고 있다.

a. 유년기, 자라고

b. 청년기, 쇠퇴하고

c. 청소년, 계속 수행되고

d. 여행자, 나타나고

e. 방랑자, 과시하고

5 아메리카 원주민 아이들은 통과 의례로 무엇을 하는가?

◎ 구문해설

2행_ The rites of passage generally refer to some difficult tasks that the youngsters would have to perform successfully in order to be considered "adults" within their group.

⇨ that은 목적격 관계대명사로 선행사는 some difficult tasks이다. 「in order to+동사원형」은 '~하기 위해'라는 의미이다.

6행_ They would have to do this alone, survive the ordeal, and then return home.

⇨ 동사 do, survive, return는 have to와 연결되어 병렬구조를 이루고 있다.

14행_ The Orthodox Jewish faith requires boys and girls to study their religious texts and memorize an enormous amount of them.

⇨ 「require+목적어+to부정사」의 문장 구조를 알아두자.

23행_ As a preteen or teen, would you like to do some rigorous activity that proves that you are not a kid anymore?

⇨ As는 전치사로 역할, 자격, 기능 등을 나타내어 '~으로서'라는 의미이다. 첫 번째 that은 주격 관계대명사로 선행사는 some rigorous activity이다. 두 번째 that은 접속사로 명사절을 이끌고 있다.

UNIT 10-2 The American Prom

◎ 정답

1. a   2. d   3. a   4. c   5. e

◎ 해석

미국 10대들은 고교 시절의 마지막과 성인으로서의 삶의 시작을 축하하는 전통이 있다. 이 특별한 행사를 고교 졸업 무도회라 부른다. 졸업 무도회는 평생 간직할 수 있는 추억을 만들어 주는 저녁 행사이다. 나이 든 사람들 다수는 50년 전에 졸업 무도회를 참석했을지라도 그날 밤의 일을 자세하게 모두 기억할 수 있다. 따라서 졸업 무도회는 정말 중요한 통과 의례이다.

졸업 무도회는 대부분 매우 공식적인 행사여서 젊은 남성은 턱시도를 입고, 젊은 여성은 격식을 차린 드레스를 입는다. 소녀들은 드레스를 사고, 소년들은 대여점에서 턱시도를 미리 확보하면서 졸업 무도회의 준비는 몇 주 전에 시작된다. 졸업 무도회가 열리는 날에 젊은 여성은 미용실에서 최신 유행에 따라 머리를 손질하고 많은 시간을 들여 화장하고 손톱을 다듬는다. 젊은 남성은 이발을 하고, 자신의 파트너가 손목에 두르거나 드레스에 달 코르사주(여성들이 가슴, 허리, 어깨에 다는 작은 꽃 장식)를 장만하느라 바쁘다.

커플은 종종 졸업 무도회 장소까지 갈 리무진을 빌리기도 한다. 몇몇 커플은 졸업 무도회에 가기 전이나 졸업 무도회가 끝난 후에 함께 저녁 식사를 하러 간다. 체육관은 낭만적으로 표현하기 위해 별이나 하트로 장식된 매우 큰 색지로 단장을 한다. 체육관은 참석자를 환영하기 위한 아치길이나 격자 장식을 리본과 꽃으로 장식함으로써 단장을 완료한다. 이곳에서 커플들은 저녁 시간 동안 사진을 찍을 것이다.

졸업 무도회는 미국에서 인기 있는 문화의 일부로서 지난 50년이 넘도록 그다지 많이 변하지 않은 전통으로 남아 있다. 성인기로 접어드는 이 중요한 단계로서 졸업 무도회는 상당히 중요시된다. 이는 한 세대에서 다음 세대까지의 공통적인 유대 관계를 제공해 주기 때문이다.

◎ 해설

1 이 글의 주요 내용은 무엇인가?

a. 통과 의례인 미국 졸업 무도회 전통

b. 미국 고교 시절의 마지막

c. 졸업 무도회에서 미국 청소년들이 하는 일

d. 졸업 무도회에 입는 복장

e. 미국 졸업 무도회를 위한 준비

2 "transformation"의 뜻에 가장 가까운 단어는 무엇인가?

a. 수송

b. 보존

c. 적용

d. 개조

e. 면적

3 미국 졸업 무도회에 대한 내용 중 사실이 아닌 것은 무엇인가?

a. 젊은 남자들은 댄스파티를 위해 정장을 차려입는다.

b. 모든 미국인들이 이 통과 의례에 참석한다.

c. 미국 고등학교 문화의 중요한 일부분이다.

d. 많은 노인들이 뚜렷하게 기억하는 행사이다.

e. 졸업 무도회에서 여학생들은 파트너가 가져온 코르사주를 한다.

4 다음 문장이 들어갈 가장 적절한 곳은 어디인가?

> 때때로 호텔에서 졸업 무도회가 열리기도 하지만, 학교 체육관에서 열리는 경우가 더욱 많다.

5 졸업 무도회에 대한 저자의 태도는 무엇인가?

a. 동정적인

b. 무관심한

c. 회의적인

d. 부정적인

e. 긍정적인

◉ 구문해설

3행_ A prom is an evening that makes memories that can last a lifetime.

⇨ 두 개의 that은 주격 관계대명사로 선행사는 각각 an evening과 memories 이다.

6행_ The prom is usually a very formal occasion requiring the young men to wear tuxedos and the young women to wear formal gowns.

⇨ 현재분사 requiring이 명사 a very formal occasion을 후치 수식하고 있다. 「require+목적어+to부정사」의 문장 구조를 알아두자.

9행_ On the day of the prom, the young ladies have their hair done in the latest fashion at a beauty salon,

⇨ 사역동사 have의 목적격 보어로 과거분사 done이 온 것으로 보아 목적어와의 관계가 수동임을 알 수 있다.

11행_ The young gentlemen are busy with haircuts and picking up the corsage that their dates will wear on the wrist or fasten to the dress.

⇨ busy with는 '~로 바쁘다'라는 뜻이다. that은 목적격 관계대명사로 선행사는 the corsage이다.

17행_ The transformation of the gym is complete with a welcoming archway or trellis laden with ribbons and flowers where couples will have their photographs taken sometime during the course of the evening.

⇨ 과거분사 laden이 archway or trellis를 후치 수식하고 있다. where는 관계부사로 a welcoming archway or trellis가 선행사이다. 사역동사 have의 목적격 보어로 과거분사 taken이 온 것으로 보아 목적어와의 관계가 수동임을 알 수 있다.

UNIT 11-1 Butterfly Beauties

◉ Pre-reading Activity

insects, outside, water

◉ 정답

1. b 2. b 3. c 4. d 5. carrying 50 times their own body weight

◉ 해석

나비는 인시류로 불리는 흥미로운 곤충이다. 모든 곤충과 마찬가지로 나비는 머리, 흉부, 복부, 두 개의 더듬이, 여섯 개의 다리를 가지고 있다. 나비는 남극 지방을 제외한 모든 대륙에서 발견되고, 전 세계적으로 대략 12,000~15,000여 종이 있으리라 추정된다.

나비는 매우 화려한 날개를 가지고 있지만, 저마다가 지닌 다양한 색깔을 즐기지 못한다. 나비는 부분적으로 색맹이기 때문에 오로지 빨간색, 초록색, 노란색만을 볼 수 있다. 나비는 아름답기는 하지만 그 아름다움이 오래 지속되지 못한다. 나비의 수명은 매우 짧은 것으로 알려져 있다. 성충이 된 일반적인 나비의 수명은 2주 정도이다. 예를 들어, 코스타리카에서 볼 수 있는 한 종(種)의 수명은 약 2일이고 길어야 10일이다. 1년이 넘도록 살 수 있는 성충 나비는 없다.

많은 나비들이 먼 거리를 이동한다. 그들은 좀 더 따뜻한 기온과 식량을 찾아 이동한다. 그들은 주로 꽃에 있는 꿀을 먹는다. 특히 제왕나비가 이주로 유명하다. 북아메리카에 서식하는 제왕나비는 가을에 4,000~4,800킬로미터 이상을 날아 따뜻한 지역으로 갔다가, 봄이 되면 다시 북쪽으로 돌아온다.

나비에게는 다채로운 아름다움 이상의 것이 있다. 나비는 우아하고 가냘픈 생물처럼 보일지 모르지만, 자기 몸무게의 50배를 들어 올릴 수 있다. 이는 성인 한 명이 승객이 가득 찬 자동차 두 대를 들어 올리는 것과 같다. 나비는 강하고, 건강하고, 놀라운 생물이고, 수분자로서도 중요한 역할을 한다. 나비는 작지만, 세상에서 가장 경이로운 동물 중 하나이다. 나비의 아름다움과 보기만 해도 놀라운 변태, 그리고 아무 걱정 없이 즐겁게 비행하는 모습이 우리의 상상력을 자극한다.

● 해설

1 이 글의 주요 내용은 무엇인가?
a. 나비의 수명
b. 나비에 대한 흥미진진한 사실
c. 나비가 볼 수 있는 색깔
d. 북아메리카에 서식하는 제왕나비
e. 나비의 놀라운 변태

2 "delicate"의 뜻에 가장 가까운 단어는 무엇인가?
a. 불결한
b. 우아한
c. 서투른
d. 비참한
e. 성가신

3 빈칸에 들어갈 가장 적절한 말은 무엇인가?
a. 그러나
b. 더욱이
c. 예를 들어
d. 게다가
e. 사실

4 다음 중 사실은 무엇인가?
a. 모든 성충 나비는 기껏해야 하루를 산다.
b. 대체로 나비는 두 개의 더듬이를 사용해서 식량을 먹을 수 있다.
c. 나비는 부분적으로 색맹이어서 검은색과 흰색만 볼 수 있다.
d. 제왕나비는 매년 가을에 따뜻한 지역으로 이주한다.
e. 전 세계에는 대략 4,800여 종의 나비가 있다.

5 "this"가 가리키는 것은 무엇인가?

● 구문해설

3행_ and it is estimated that there are approximately
가주어 _____ 진주어
12,000~15,000 species of butterflies in the world

7행_ Beautiful as they are, their beauty cannot last long.
➾ Beautiful as they are는 Though they are beautiful로 바꿔 쓸 수 있다. as는 접속사로 양보를 나타내어 '~이기는 하지만'이라는 의미이다.

10행_ one species found in Costa Rica has a life expectancy of about two days and lives ten days at the most
➾ one species와 found 사이에 「관계대명사+be동사」가 생략되었다고 생각하면 문장 구조를 쉽게 이해할 수 있다. at the most는 '많아야, 기껏해야'라는 의미이다.

19행_ This would be like an adult human lifting two heavy cars full of people.
➾ 현재분사 lifting이 an adult human을 후치 수식하고 있다. cars와 full 사이에 「관계대명사+be동사」가 생략되었다고 생각하면 문장 구조를 쉽게 이해할 수 있다.

UNIT 11-2 The Deceptive Moth

● Pre-reading Activity

1. T   2. T   3. F

● 정답

1. c   2. a   3. d   4. e   5. They live off the reserves of fat from when they were in the caterpillar stage of their lives.

● 해석

홍콩에서 광둥어를 쓰는 사람들이 그것을 가리키는 이름이 있는데, 해석하면 뱀 머리 나방이다. 이탈리아인은 이것을 파팔라 코브라라 부른다. 날개의 무늬를 보면 사람들이 이것의 이름으로 뱀, 코브라, 기타 뱀을 가리키는 단어를 쓰는지 쉽게 알 수 있다. 우리들 대부분은 아틀라스 나방으로 알고 있을 뿐이다. 이 나방은 세계에서 가장 크다. 그 이유는 날개 길이가 30센티미터에 달하기 때문일 것이다.

이 커다란 나방은 열대 동남아시아에서만 찾아볼 수 있는데 대개는 말레이 군도와 인도의 일부 지역에 분포해 있다. 싱가포르에는 이 나방이 11월과 12월에 많다. 아틀라스 나방은 날개에 뱀 머리를 닮은 무늬가 있고 색깔은 주로 황갈색에서 밤색이다. 이런 모습을 띠는 목적은 아마도 포식자를 피하기 위해서일 것이다. 한 번 생각해 보자! 공격하는 새나 기타 포식자가 아틀라스 나방을 덮치기 전에 한 번 더 생각할 것이 분명하다. 남의 눈을 속이는 위장에 인간조차 겁을 먹어 대부분의 사람들은 아틀라스 나방을 만지려 하지도 않는다.

인도에서는 다르기는 하지만 같은 과(科)에 속하는 무리인 누에나방처럼 아틀라스 나방의 고치로 비단실을 만들기도 한다. 이 비단실은 누에나방의 비단실보다 더 견고하다고 여겨진다. 타이완에서 아틀라스 나방의 고치는 지갑과 핸드백을 만드는 데 쓰인다.

아틀라스 나방이 아름답고 교활하기는 하지만, 수명을 길게 누리지는 못한다. 실제로 성충 아틀라스 나방의 수명은 2주가 채 못 된다. 아틀라스 나방은 먹고 싶어도 먹을 수가 없다. 입이 없기 때문이다. 그저 애벌레 단계에 있을 때 비축해 둔 지방을 먹고 살 뿐이다. 성충 아틀라스 나방이 하는 일은 단순히 수컷과

암컷이 서로의 짝을 찾아 짝짓기를 하고, 알을 낳고, 그런 후에 곧 죽는 것이다.

○ 해설

1 이 글의 주요 내용은 무엇인가?
　a. 아틀라스 나방에게 주어진 이름들
　b. 아틀라스 나방의 서식지와 음식
　c. 아틀라스 나방에 대한 흥미로운 사실
　d. 아틀라스 나방의 크기와 외형
　e. 아틀라스 나방 고치의 유용함

2 "deceptive"의 뜻에 가장 가까운 단어는 무엇인가?
　a. 오해하게 하는
　b. 흥미로운
　c. 논쟁의 여지가 있는
　d. 자만하는
　e. 이상한

3 빈칸에 들어갈 가장 적절한 말은 무엇인가?
　a. 대부분의 사람들이 아틀라스 나방의 비열한 습성을 좋아한다.
　b. 대부분의 사람들이 아틀라스 나방을 보려고 동물원에 간다.
　c. 많은 사람이 아틀라스 나방을 집에서 키우는 것을 좋아한다.
　d. 대부분의 사람들이 아틀라스 나방을 만지는 것조차 싫어한다.
　e. 대부분의 사람들이 정글에서 아틀라스 나방을 보는 것을 즐긴다.

4 다음 중 사실이 아닌 것은 무엇인가?
　a. 포식자는 아틀라스 나방을 쉽게 공격할 수 없다.
　b. 아틀라스 나방은 산란기가 끝나고 곧 죽는다.
　c. 아틀라스 나방의 날개 무늬는 적을 혼동시키기 위한 것으로 여겨진다.
　d. 아틀라스 나방은 뱀을 닮은 무늬 때문에 독특한 이름으로 불린다.
　e. 아틀라스 나방의 비단실은 누에나방의 비단실만큼 견고하지 않다.

5 성충 아틀라스 나방은 입이 없이 어떻게 생존할 수 있는가?

○ 구문해설

3행_ it is easy to see why there are people who put words like snake, cobra, or some other serpent title in its name

⇨ it은 가주어. to see 이하는 진주어이다. 관계사 why 이하는 동사 see의 목적어 역할을 하는 명사절을 이끌고 있다. who는 주격 관계대명사로 선행사는 people이다.

9행_ The Atlas moths are commonly tawny to maroon in color with patterns on its wings that resemble a snake's head.

⇨ tawny to maroon in color는 '색상이 황갈색에서 밤색까지'라는 의미이다. that은 주격 관계대명사로 선행사는 patterns이다.

25행_ the males and females need to find each other, mate, lay eggs, and die shortly thereafter

⇨ find, mate, lay, die는 need to와 연결되어 동사원형으로 병렬관계를 이루고 있다. 「need to+동사원형」은 '~할 필요가 있다'라는 뜻이다.

UNIT 12-1　The Enhanced Greenhouse Effect

○ 정답

1. b　2. d　3. a　4. d　5. b

○ 해석

아마도 오늘날 가장 지속적이면서 원상태로 되돌릴 수 있는 가능성이 가장 적은 세계적 문제는 바로 강화된 온실효과일 것이다. 이 효과는 지나치게 많은 양의 이산화탄소, 메탄, 프레온 가스, 그리고 지구의 대기 중으로 분출되는 10여 가지가 넘는 기타 기체로 인해 발생한다. 이 중에서 이산화탄소가 가장 비중 있는 역할을 한다. 대기에서 차지하는 이산화탄소의 양은 늘어난 석탄, 석유, 기타 화석 연료의 연소로 인해 1800년대 중반 이후로 꾸준히 증가하고 있다.

1970년대에 들어 전 세계적으로 대기 중의 이산화탄소의 농도는 대략 320ppm이었던 반면에, 현재 이산화탄소 농도는 380ppm까지 증가했다. 온실 가스, 특히 이산화탄소의 배출이 현재 추세대로 억제되지 않고 계속 증가한다면 과거 어느 때보다 훨씬 큰 기후 변화가 일어날지도 모른다. 이렇게 되면 자연 생태계, 인간과 동물의 건강, 세계 자원의 분포가 상당히 바뀔 것이다. 게다가 강화된 온실효과와 그로 인해 발생하는 지구 온난화로 극빙이 급속히 녹아 그로 인해 해수면이 상승하고, 결과적으로 해안 지역과 도시에 물이 범람할 것이다. 이런 현상으로 생겨나는 여러 위험에 대한 해결책을 찾기 위해서는 세계 정책을 고안해 내야 할지 모른다.

이런 딜레마와 더불어 우리가 직면한 또 다른 문제는, 이러한 현상이 자연발생적이고 정상적이라고 말하는 사람이 많다는 점이다. 애석하게도 이런 사람들은 소수의 과학자들만을 믿고 있으며 이러한 자연 재해 현상을 과학적으로 명백히 입증하고 있는 압도적으로 많은 과학자들의 주장을 무시한다. 우리는 과학 시간에 이러한 상황을 반전할 수 있도록 도와줄 현재와 미래의 지도자를 더욱 잘 훈련시켜야 한다.

○ 해설

1 두 번째 문단의 주요 내용은 무엇인가?
　a. 화석 연료를 줄이기 위한 우리의 노력
　b. 이산화탄소의 증가로 인해 발생한 현상

c. 미래에 우리가 지구 온난화를 해결할 수 있는 묘책

d. 다가올 미래에 이용할 대체 에너지

e. 대기 중의 이산화탄소 농도가 증가한 이유

2 빈칸에 들어갈 가장 적절한 단어는 무엇인가?

	(A)	(B)
a.	~이기는 하지만	이례적인
b.	~임에도 불구하고	자연스러운
c.	만약 ~한다면	드문
d.	~에 반해서	정상적인
e.	~하는 동안	비정상적인

3 "disregarding"의 뜻에 가장 가까운 단어는 무엇인가?

a. 무시하는

b. 혐오스러운

c. 의존하는

d. 지지하는

e. 존경하는

4 강화된 온실효과의 주요 원인은 무엇인가?

a. 지구 온난화에 대한 해결책의 부족

b. 극빙의 해빙과 해수면의 상승

c. 소수의 과학자들의 말에 귀를 기울이는 무지한 사람들

d. 대기 중으로의 이산화탄소의 배출

e. 자연 생태계와 지구 건강의 변화

5 이 글에서 유추할 수 있는 내용은 무엇인가?

a. 많은 회사가 대체 연료를 사용할 것이다.

b. 우리의 환경을 위한 강력한 세계적 정책이 필요하다.

c. 이산화탄소의 대기 농도는 예측하기 어렵다.

d. 지구 온난화와 온실효과는 연관성이 없다.

e. 강화된 온실효과는 지구의 대기 중에서 발생하는 자연스러운 현상이다.

○ 구문해설

7행_ The amount of this gas in the atmosphere has risen steadily since the mid-1800s as a result of the combustion of coal, oil, and other fossil fuels on an ever-widening scale.

⇨ amount of는 일반적으로 불가산명사와 쓰여 양을 나타낸다. has risen은 현재완료 용법 중 계속을 나타내고 있다. as a result of는 '~의 결과로'라는 뜻이다.

12행_ If present trends in the emission of greenhouse gases, particularly CO2, continue to rise unchecked, climatic changes larger than any ever previously experienced may occur.

⇨ 접속사 If가 이끄는 절은 가정법이 아닌 조건절이며, 주절의 주어는 climatic changes이다.

15행_ the enhanced greenhouse effect and subsequent global warming could continue to cause the rapid melting of polar ice, resulting in a rise in sea levels and the consequent flooding of coastal areas and cities.

⇨ resulting 이하는 분사구문으로 의미상의 주어는 the enhanced greenhouse effect and subsequent global warming이다.

20행_ Another problem facing us with this dilemma is that many people are saying this phenomenon is a natural occurrence, and it is natural.

⇨ facing은 현재분사로 명사 Another problem을 후치 수식하고 있다. that 은 접속사로 명사절을 이끌며, 이 명사절은 주격 보어 역할을 하고 있다. saying 과 this phenomenon 사이에는 접속사 that이 생략되었다.

UNIT 12-2 Environmental Solutions

○ 정답

1. c 2. e 3. a 4. b 5. Gas, coal, and other pollution-creating fuels will go by the wayside., People will save money and a green revolution will take place.

○ 해석

전 세계의 환경 문제를 일으키는 가장 큰 원인은 우리의 에너지 선택이다. 우리는 자동차에 연료를 공급하기 위해 휘발유를 태운다. 우리는 석탄을 연소해서 공장을 운영하고 전기 발전소에 동력을 공급한다. 우리가 약 수십 년간 시종일관 알아왔던 많은 다른 기술이 있다. 이런 기술이 자동차를 운행하고 집을 난방하고 전기를 공급할 것이다. 이런 기술은 깨끗하다. 아니 비교적 깨끗하다고 말하는 것이 적절할지도 모른다. 이런 에너지원은 태양력과 조력에서부터 사람들이 매일 새롭게 생각해내는 수많은 녹색 기술의 이용에까지 이른다.

애석하게도, 거대 정유회사와 그들을 위해 일하는 로비스트, 그리고 국제 다국적 복합기업에 굴복하는 나약한 정부 지도자가 이런 혁신과 녹색 기술을 억제하고 있다. 거대 정유회사는 일단 이런 신기술이 이용 가능해지면, 가스, 석탄, 기타 오염을 유발하는 연료가 밀려날 것이라는 사실을 오래 전부터 알고 있었다.

최근에 몇몇 녹색 기술 운동이 일어나고 있지만, 많은 가정에서는 진전 속도가 늦은 것에 지쳐 독자적으로 녹색 기술 운동을 추진하고 있다. 점점 더 많은 가정에서 자신의 집에 저비용 에너지 기계를 설치하는 방법을 배우고 있다. 그들은 태양열 주택을 자체적으로 짓고, 자신의 집과 때때로 자동차에 동력을 제

공할 작은 풍차와 기타 도구를 설치하고 있다. 자체적으로 무료로 에너지를 발생하는 장치와 기계를 설치하고 있는 선구적인 가정은 더욱 밝고 깨끗한 미래로 향하는 길을 주도하고 있다. 이것이 깨끗하고 저비용의 에너지 기술이 확산되는 방식이라 생각된다. 이렇게 녹색 혁명은 정부나 대기업에 의해서가 아니라 선구적인 개인에 의해 일어날 것이다.

○ 해설

1 이 글의 주제는 무엇인가?
 a. 우리는 대체 연료 차량을 사용해야 한다.
 b. 우리는 대체 연료를 발명할 방법을 찾아야 한다.
 c. 우리는 대체 연료를 사용함으로써 지구를 구할 수 있다.
 d. 점점 더 많은 가정이 친환경 주택을 짓는 법을 배우고 있다.
 e. 정부는 에너지를 절약하기 위해 대기업과 협력해야 한다.

2 "harnessing"의 뜻에 가장 가까운 단어는 무엇인가?
 a. 방출하다
 b. 소비하다
 c. 억제하다
 d. 진척시키다
 e. 활용하다

3 빈칸에 들어갈 가장 적절한 단어는 무엇인가?
 a. 불행하게도
 b. 개의치 않는
 c. 그러므로
 d. 마찬가지로
 e. 다행히

4 에너지 선구자들에 대한 저자의 태도는 무엇인가?
 a. 중립적인
 b. 희망적인
 c. 풍자적인
 d. 슬퍼하는
 e. 부정적인

5 녹색 기술이 실행될 가능성이 증가하면 어떤 일이 일어날까?

○ 구문해설

3행_ there are many other technologies that we have known about for decades
⇒ that은 목적격 관계대명사로 선행사는 many other technologies이다.

4행_ These technologies will run our cars, heat our homes, and provide our electricity.
⇒ run, heat, provide는 조동사 will과 연결되어 병렬관계를 이루고 있다.

11행_ The big oil companies have known for quite a while that once these new technologies become available,

gas, coal, and other pollution-creating fuels will go by the wayside.
⇒ that은 접속사로 명사절을 이끌어 have known의 목적어 역할을 하고 있다. that 이하의 명사절은 다시 once가 이끄는 부사절과 gas, coal, and other pollution-creating fuels가 주어인 주절로 구분되어 있다.

14행_ While there has been some recent movement into green technologies, a lot of families are tired of the slow pace and are going it alone.
⇒ 접속사 while은 주절과 반대 · 비교 · 대조를 나타내어 '그런데, 한편으로는' 등의 의미를 가지고 있다. go it alone은 '혼자서 행하다'라는 의미이다.

18행_ These pioneering families who are building their own free energy devices and machines are leading the way into a brighter and cleaner future.
⇒ 위 문장의 주어는 These pioneering families이고 본동사는 두 번째 are 이다. who는 주격 관계대명사이다.

23행_ We can expect that this is how clean, low-cost energy technologies will spread.
⇒ that은 접속사로 동사 expect의 목적어를 이끌고 있다. 관계사 how가 이끄는 명사절은 주격 보어 역할을 하고 있다.

UNIT 13-1 CIA Gadgets—Past and Present

○ Pre-reading Activity

1. T   2. T   3. F

○ 정답

1. a   2. c   3. c   4. c   5. d

○ 해석

아마도 영화, 책, 신문에서 사람들이 CIA에 대해 하는 말을 들어봤을 것이다. CIA가 중앙 정보국을 의미한다는 것도 알고 있을 것이다. CIA는 미국 정보기관으로 할리우드에 의해 스파이와 그들의 위험한 생활방식이 알려져 유명해졌다. 많은 사람들이 매력을 느끼는 그들의 삶 중에서 하나는 스파이가 사용하는 도구와 장치이다.

CIA는 요원들이 더 이상 사용하지 않는 장치를 보여 주려고 대중에게 박물관을 공개했다. 박물관에는 발명가의 창의성을 보여 주는 독창적인 장비들이 많이 전시되어 있다. CIA가 베트남 전쟁 중 아시아의 정글에서 사용했던 도청 장치는 동물의 배설물처럼 생겼다. 아무도 동물 배설물을 줍지는 않을 것이므로 염탐 대상인 군인들에게 한 번도 발견되지 않았다. 또 다른 정글 도청 장치는 원격 조종 잠자리였다. 스파이는 도청하고 싶은 곳에 원격 조종기로 잠자리를 보냈다. 잠자리는 공중을 날아다니면서 대화 내용을 녹음한다. CIA가 사진이 필요하면 스파이는 소형 카메라를 비둘기의 가슴에 매단다. 일부 카메라는 비둘기에게 너무 무거워서 실패작이었다. 비둘기들은 사진을 찍기 위해 머리 위로 날아다니는 대신에 그저 걸어 다니기만 했다. 좀 더 최근에 사용된 일부 기술 또한 흥미롭다. 스파이들에게는 전쟁이나 충돌이 일어난 지역에 뿌리는 특별한 분말이 있다. 이 분말은 적의 움직임을 감지해서 그들이 어디에 있는지, 어디로 가고 있는지 CIA에 전달한다. CIA가 당신의 사진을 갖고 있다면 어떻게 될까? 조심해야 한다. 그렇지 않으면 스파이들이 당신을 찾아낼 것이다. 스파이들이 사진을 인터넷에 연결시키면 소프트웨어가 당신과 일치하는 코나 턱, 기타 신체 부위를 가진 사람을 찾기 위해 웹과 개인 컴퓨터까지 조사할 것이다. 정말 멋진 물건이 아닌가?

◯ 해설

1 이 글의 주요 내용은 무엇인가?
  a. CIA가 사용하는 멋진 스파이 장비
  b. CIA의 중요한 임무인 스파이 행위
  c. 미국의 정부 기관으로서의 CIA
  d. CIA를 위해 일하는 뛰어난 스파이
  e. 최신 스파이 장비를 전시한 박물관

2 "ingenious"의 뜻에 가장 가까운 단어는 무엇인가?
  a. 사소한
  b. 서투른
  c. 뛰어난
  d. 무능한
  e. 진부한

3 빈칸에 들어갈 가장 적절한 말은 무엇인가?
  a. 자신의 짝을 찾는다
  b. 적을 생포한다
  c. 대화를 녹음한다
  d. 적과 휴전한다
  e. 소음을 일으켜 군인들의 주의를 산만하게 한다

4 "they"가 가리키는 것은 무엇인가?
  a. 사진
  b. CIA
  c. 비둘기
  d. 카메라
  e. 비둘기의 가슴

5 이 글에서 유추할 수 있는 내용은 무엇인가?
  a. 박물관은 진부한 스파이 도구를 소장하고 있다
  b. 일부 현대 스파이 장비는 시중에서 구할 수 있다.

  c. 전쟁 중에 도청은 법에 어긋난다.
  d. CIA는 나쁜 사람을 잡기 위해 얼굴 인식 소프트웨어를 사용하기도 한다.
  e. CIA의 장비는 주로 개인 정보를 얻기 위해 사용되었다.

◯ 구문해설

2행_ The CIA is the American governmental <u>agency</u> <u>made</u> famous by Hollywood because of its spies and their dangerous lifestyles.
⇨ agency와 made 사이에 「관계대명사+be동사」가 생략되었다고 생각하면 문장 구조를 쉽게 이해할 수 있다.

4행_ <u>One</u> of the aspects of their lives (<u>that</u> many people are attracted to) <u>is</u> the tools and gadgets <u>that</u> the spies use.
⇨ 첫 번째 that은 목적격 관계대명사로 선행사는 the aspects이다. 위 문장의 주어는 one이고, is가 본동사이다. 두 번째 that 역시 목적격 관계대명사로, 선행사는 the tools and gadgets이다.

15행_ Some of these cameras were a failure <u>in that</u> the cameras were too heavy for the pigeons,
⇨ in that은 '~이라는 점에서, ~이므로, ~이기 때문에(because, since)'라는 뜻이다.

20행_ The dust picks up the enemy movement and <u>tells</u> the CIA <u>where they are</u> and <u>where they are going</u>.
⇨ 동사 tell의 직접목적어로 두 개의 간접의문문이 쓰였다.

UNIT 13-2 The Copenhagen Wheel

◯ 정답

1. d   2. e   3. b   4. d   5. to promote cycling and protect the environment

◯ 해석

대기 오염을 측정하는 자료 수집기와 더불어 손잡이에 아이폰이 달려 있고 항법 장치와 건강 정보를 제공하는 자전거를 상상할 수 있는가? 이는 '코펜하겐 휠'로 알려져 있는 새로 나온 이 역동적인 자전거가 가진 기능의 일부에 불과하다. 이 자전거의 매우 독특한 특징은 뒷바퀴에 부착된 빨간 바퀴통인데, 이 바퀴통 안에 있는 자전거의 중심부가 동력을 저장하고, 속도를 끌어올리고, 자전거 타는 사람의 운동을 기록하고, 공기와 주변 환경으로부터 자료를 수집한다. 수집된 자료가 공공 기관의 웹사이트에 입력되면 도시 거주민들은 그날의 대기 상태가 어떠한지 알 수 있다.

코펜하겐 휠은 미국 매사추세츠 공과대학(MIT)에서 제작되었다. 이것은 우리 도시의 기반 시설 중 한 부분인 생활용품에 '지능'을 넣는 일을 하는 MIT의 한 연구소에서 개발되었다. MIT 연구자들은 코펜하겐 기후 변화 회담을 선택해서 새 자전거 바퀴를 선보였고, 초기 반응은 매우 긍정적이었다.

간단하게 정의해 보자면, 코펜하겐 휠 프로젝트의 목적은 사람들이 갈 수 있는 거리의 범위를 넓혀서 자전거타기를 장려하는 것이다. 게다가 제조업체는 자전거를 좀 더 부드럽게 탈 수 있게 제작하여 자전거를 편안하게 탈 수 있도록 해서 오르막이 더 이상 문제가 되지 않도록 했다. 또한 이 새로운 자전거는 배기가스 배출을 줄여 환경을 보호하는 데 안성맞춤이다. 따라서 많은 대도시에서는 거주민들이 출퇴근할 때 이토록 혁신적인 두 발 운송수단을 사용하도록 장려하는 계획을 세우고 있다. 코펜하겐 휠 프로젝트의 책임자인 크리스틴 오트람은 이 새로운 자전거가 21세기로의 스마트 트랜스포테이션을 주도하는 데 유용할 것으로 기대하고 있다. 그녀는 다수의 주요 대도시에 사는 거주민에게 이런 형태의 자전거 타기를 장려해서 이익을 보리라 확신한다.

○ 해설

1 이 글의 주요 내용은 무엇인가?
  a. 자전거에 부착될 새로운 바퀴
  b. 새로운 자전거를 발명한 MIT에 소속된 팀
  c. 자전거 사용을 증진하기 위한 실용적인 방법
  d. 최첨단적인 특징을 보유한 환경 친화적인 자전거
  e. 대도시에서 혁신적인 자전거가 자동차를 대체하게 될 방식

2 "show off"의 뜻에 가장 가까운 단어는 무엇인가?
  a. 구입하다
  b. 규제하다
  c. 조직하다
  d. 조립하다
  e. 설명하다

3 이 글에서 유추할 수 있는 내용은 무엇인가?
  a. 자전거를 타는 사람이 늘어날수록 자동차를 타는 사람도 늘어날 것이다.
  b. 자전거를 타는 사람이 늘어날수록 도로 교통량은 줄어들 것이다.
  c. 자전거를 타는 사람이 늘어날수록 환경오염이 심해질 것이다.
  d. 자전거를 타는 사람이 늘어날수록 거리에서 발생하는 말다툼이 늘어날 것이다.
  e. 자전거를 타는 사람이 늘어날수록 거주민들은 지하철을 자주 탈 것이다.

4 빈칸에 들어갈 가장 적절한 단어는 무엇인가?

> 코펜하겐 휠이라 불리는 독창적인 자전거는 MIT에서 발명했다. 그것은 사람들이 자전거를 탈 수 있는 범위를 늘려서 자전거 타기를 권장하고 궁극적으로 환경에 유익할 것이다.

  a. 만들었다, 감소시켜서
  b. 만들었다, 맞춰서
  c. 보여 주었다, 잘라서
  d. 발명했다, 늘려서
  e. 바꿨다, 고려해서

5 코펜하겐 휠 프로젝트의 목적은 무엇인가?

○ 구문해설

4행_ The most distinctive feature of this bike is its red hub on the rear wheel, where the brain of the bike stores power, boosts speed, monitors the rider's exercise, and collects data from the air and the environment.
➡ where는 관계부사로 선행사는 its red hub이다. 동사 stores, boosts, monitors, collects는 주어 the brain과 연결되어 병렬관계를 이루고 있다.

7행_ The data that is collected is put onto a public website so city residents can find out what their urban atmosphere is like during the day.
➡ 주격 관계대명사 that은 형용사절을 이끌어 주어이자 선행사인 The data를 수식하고 있다. what은 명사절을 이끌어 동사 find out의 목적어 역할을 한다.

10행_ It is developed by a part of MIT that is putting "intelligence" into everyday items that are a part of the infrastructure of our cities.
➡ 밑줄 친 that은 둘 다 주격 관계대명사로 선행사는 각각 a part of MIT와 everyday items이다.

17행_ This new bicycle is also perfect for protecting the environment by reducing emissions, and many big cities are making plans to encourage their residents to use this innovative two-wheeler when they commute to and from work.
➡ 전치사 by는 수단·방법·원인·작용 등을 나타내어 '~에 의해서, ~으로'라는 의미이다. 「encourage+목적어+to부정사」의 문장 구조를 알아두자. they는 their residents를 나타낸다.

UNIT 14-1 The Berlin Wall and Its Legacy

○ 정답

1. b 2. c 3. a 4. b 5. c

○ 해석

독일의 수도를 분단했던 베를린 장벽은 2차 세계대전이 끝나고 가속화된 세계 양대 초강대국(미국과 소비에트 연방) 사이의 냉전이 불러온 긴장을 상징하게 되었다. 동독은 공산주의 국가가

되었지만, 서독은 매일의 사건을 통제하는 미국의 지지를 받는 자본주의 국가가 되었다.

현재 알려진 사실에 따르면, 소비에트 연방의 지도자인 조셉 스탈린은 공산주의 위성국으로 독일 전역을 포함시키려는 계획을 세웠지만, 미국과 기타 연합국이 독일에 계속 주둔했던 관계로 그 계획을 실현시키지 못했다. 베를린은 동독에 위치해 있었음에도 전쟁에서 승리한 연합국에 의해 도시가 나뉘었다. 서구 연합국인 미국, 영국, 프랑스는 서베를린을 형성했고, 소비에트 연방은 동베를린을 형성했다. 전쟁이 끝나고 20년 동안 두 도시 간의 통행이 비록 엄격하게 제한되기는 했지만, 실제로 장벽이 세워질 때보다는 느슨했다. 베를린은 특히 야심을 품은 젊은이들이 좀 더 개방적인 서독으로 건너가기 위한 최적의 장소로 여겨졌다.

동독인과 그 배후의 소비에트 연방 사람들은 많은 사람들이 동독에서 빠져나가고 있다는 사실을 알고 점차 당혹감을 느꼈다. 그래서 1961년에 베를린 장벽을 세우기 시작했다. 베를린은 처음에는 가시 달린 철조망으로, 그런 다음 더욱 튼튼한 방비 시설로 인해 분리되었다. 그 후에 많은 가족들이 흩어졌고 서베를린은 공산주의 국가인 동독 안에서 섬처럼 고립되었다.

베를린 장벽은 공산주의와 자본주의를 가르는 비유적인 의미로 철의 장막을 나타내는 물리적 상징물이었다. 미하일 고르바초프가 소비에트 사회주의 공화국 연방의 대통령이 되고 나서야 비로소 공산주의와 자본주의 국가의 관계가 완화되었다. 고르바초프는 미국을 방문하고, 세계 지도자들과 친분을 쌓았으며, 동구 연합의 경제를 개혁했다. 마침내 1989년에 장벽이 완전히 붕괴될 것이라는 성명(聲明)이 발표되었고, 동베를린 사람들은 다가올 통일을 축하하기 위해 베를린 장벽을 타고 넘어 서베를린으로 갔다.

● 해설

1 이 글의 주요 내용은 무엇인가?
   a. 초강대국 사이에 벌어진 냉전 체제
   b. 베를린 장벽의 시작과 끝
   c. 냉전을 종식시킨 고르바초프의 공헌
   d. 공산주의와 자본주의의 첨예한 갈등
   e. 베를린 장벽이 독일을 두 나라로 분리한 방법

2 "restricted"의 뜻에 가장 가까운 단어는 무엇인가?
   a. 해방하다
   b. 유죄를 선고하다
   c. 억제하다
   d. 극복하다
   e. 선언하다

3 빈칸에 들어갈 가장 적절한 말은 무엇인가?
   a. 베를린 장벽은 완전히 붕괴될 것이다.

b. 베를린 장벽이 가능한 빨리 재건될 것이다.
   c. 베를린 장벽은 낮 동안 일시적으로 공개할 것이다.
   d. 누구라도 비자가 있으면 베를린 장벽을 통과할 수 있다.
   e. 동독에서 서베를린으로의 접근이 쉬워질 것이다.

4 다음 중 사실은 무엇인가?
   a. 동독인과 소비에트 연방을 지지하는 사람들이 베를린 장벽을 세웠다.
   b. 많은 서독인이 거대한 야망을 품고 동독으로 떠났다.
   c. 2차 세계대전이 끝나고 독일은 두 개의 국가로 분리되었다.
   d. 자본주의 국가가 된 서베를린은 베를린 장벽으로 고립되었다.
   e. 2차 세계대전의 승전국은 미국, 영국, 프랑스, 소비에트 연방이었다.

5 이 글의 성격은 어떠한가?
   a. 향수를 불러일으키는
   b. 설득적인
   c. 정보를 제공하는
   d. 비교하는
   e. 논쟁적인

● 구문해설

5행_ It is now known that the Soviet leader, Joseph Stalin, had plans to include all of Germany as one of the Communist satellites, but that would never come to be as the U.S.A. and other Allied countries stayed in the region.

⇨ It은 문장의 가주어, that은 진주어이다. 첫 번째 as는 전치사로 '~으로서'라는 의미로 쓰여 역할·자격·기능 등을 나타낸다. 두 번째 as는 접속사로 이유를 나타내어 '~ 때문에'라는 의미이다.

10행_ For a couple of decades after the war, passage between the two separated Berlins, though severely restricted, was more relaxed than it would eventually become.

⇨ 접속사 though 다음에 「주어(passage)+be동사」가 생략되었다. it은 passage between the two separated Berlins를 대신해 쓰이고 있다.

14행_ The East Germans and their Soviet backers knew the country was losing a lot of people, and this was becoming an embarrassment.

⇨ 동사 knew와 the country 사이에 접속사 that이 생략되었다. the country was losing a lot of people은 동사 knew의 목적어 역할을 하고 있다.

20행_ Only when Mikhail Gorbachev became the head of the Union of Soviet Socialist Republics, was there a thawing of relations.

⇨ was there a thawing of relations는 there was thawing of relations가 도치된 문장이다. 문두에 부정의 표현이나 only 등이 강조되어 문장 앞으로 나올 경우, 주어와 동사가 도치된다.

UNIT 14-2　Tiananmen Square

○ Pre-reading Activity

China, North Korea, Vietnam, Laos, Cuba

○ 정답

1. e　2. e　3. a　4. c　5. c

○ 해석

덩샤오핑은 마오쩌둥이 사망하고 나서 중국 공산당의 주석이 되었다. 마오쩌둥의 잔인한 억압이 있은 후에 실시된 덩샤오핑의 경제 자유 정책으로 희망의 분위기가 조성되었다. 동구 공산권의 몰락으로 많은 중국인들이 중국에서도 같은 개혁, 즉 민주화와 좀 더 자유로운 자본주의 사회가 되기를 기대하기 시작했다.

덩샤오핑은 전통적인 마르크스주의와 현대화를 요구하는 압력 사이에서 타협점을 찾았다. 그는 자유 시장 자본주의가 들어설 수 있도록 일부 대도시를 특별 경제 구역으로 지정했다. 그는 중국식 자본주의가 특별 경제 구역에서 어떻게 작용하는지 알아볼 의도였고, 이러한 정책은 대체적으로 긍정적인 결과를 거두었다. 이는 시장 경제와 일부 정치적 자유 정책을 점진적으로 실시해서 마오쩌둥이 조직한 체제를 완화시켰다.

하지만 일부 학생과 지식인은 이러한 개혁이 민주화에 대한 그들의 열망에 부응하지 못했고, 중국은 자국의 정치 체제를 바꿔야 한다고 생각했다. 그들은 중국 개혁이 고르바초프가 소비에트 연방에서 이룩하고 있는 개혁을 반영해야 한다고 생각했다. 중국 공산당 총서기 후야오방도 경제 변화와 정부 구조 내에서 민주적인 개혁에 대한 요구를 표명했다. 하지만, 그는 결국 비판을 받고 공직에서 쫓겨났고 얼마 지나지 않아 사망했다.

많은 중국인은 민주주의와 언론의 자유가 경제 개혁과 함께 실시되리라 생각했다. 따라서 후야오방의 사망은 전국적으로 시위가 발생하게 된 계기가 되었다. 군중의 압력으로 인해 당 지도부가 움직이리라 기대하면서, 천안문 광장에 집결한 시위자들은 중국 공산당에 대한 불만을 표출했다. 하지만, 탱크로 군중에게 발포하라는 명령이 내려졌고 많은 사람이 체포되었다. 시위는 7주간 계속되었고, 엄청나게 많은 사람이 죽었다. 이 사건은 민주주의를 실현하려는 희망을 짓밟는 행동으로 기억될 것이다.

○ 해설

1 이 글의 주요 내용은 무엇인가?
- a. 덩샤오핑의 개혁에 대한 시위자들의 전폭적인 지지
- b. 천안문 광장에 집결한 시위대에 대한 중국 공산당의 탄압
- c. 민주주의와 경제 개혁에 대한 오랜 염원
- d. 후야오방의 갑작스러운 죽음을 애도하는 엄청난 조문 물결
- e. 천안문 광장 시위의 배경과 역사적 중요성

2 "reaped"의 뜻에 가장 가까운 단어는 무엇인가??
- a. 옹호하다
- b. 단념하다
- c. 재생하다
- d. 낙담하다
- e. 달성하다

3 빈칸에 들어갈 가장 적절한 단어는 무엇인가?
- a. 그러나
- b. 그러므로
- c. 즉
- d. 예를 들어
- e. 더욱이

4 다음 중 사실은 무엇인가?
- a. 덩샤오핑은 고르바초프의 이념에 지대한 영향을 받았다.
- b. 시위자들은 대부분 마오쩌둥의 사망에 자극을 받았다.
- c. 변화는 시위자들이 바란 만큼 빨리 이뤄지지 않았을 것이다.
- d. 덩샤오핑 시대에는 언론의 자유가 보장되었다.
- e. 천안문 광장의 대량학살은 중국 공산당의 정치 체계의 변화를 일으켰다.

5 빈칸에 들어갈 가장 적절한 단어는 무엇인가?

> 많은 중국인들은 중국이 <u>민주주의</u> 국가가 되기를 바랐지만, 그들의 기대는 이뤄지지 않았다. 그 결과, 정치적, 경제적 개혁을 부르짖는 시위가 천안문 광장에서 벌어졌고, 중국 정부는 시위자들을 <u>탄압했다</u>.

- a. 공산주의, 경멸했다
- b. 중립적인, 끌어내렸다
- c. 민주적인, 탄압했다
- d. 자유로운, 지불했다
- e. 관료주의, 굴복시켰다

○ 구문해설

7행_ He placed some large cities as special economic zones where free-market capitalism could take place.

⇨ 동사 place는 '~를 지정하다, 임명하다'라는 의미이다. where는 관계부사로 in which로 바꿔 쓸 수 있다.

12행_ some students and intellectuals thought that the reforms were not enough to meet their desire for democratization and that China needed to change its political system.

⇨ 두 개의 that절이 동사 thought의 목적어 역할을 하고 있다.

14행_ They believed Chinese reforms should mirror the reforms Gorbachev was making in the Soviet Union.

⇨ believed와 Chinese 사이에 접속사 that이 생략되었다. the reforms와 Gorbachev 사이에 목적격 관계대명사가 생략되었다.

20행_ Protestors gathered at Tiananman Square to express their displeasure with the Chinese Communist Party, expecting that the pressure of the public would move the party leaders.
⇨ to express는 to부정사의 부사적 용법으로 목적을 나타낸다. expecting은 분사구문으로 의미상의 주어는 protestors이다.

24행_ This event would be remembered as the crushing of the hopes of democracy.
⇨ as는 전치사로 쓰여 '~으로서'의 뜻으로 역할 · 자격 · 기능 · 성질 등을 나타낸다.

UNIT 15-1　Does the Earth Breathe?

● **Pre-reading Activity**

species, exist, interacts

● **정답**

1. d　2. c　3. c　4. e　5. b

● **해석**

러시아의 천체 물리학자는 지구가 실제로 생명체처럼 호흡하는지 연구하고 있다. 일부 사람들에게는 약간 놀라운 사실이지만, 그들은 지구가 실제로 호흡한다고 결론을 내렸다. 그들은 인간, 나무, 식물, 박테리아, 그리고 지구가 부양하는 그 밖의 모든 유형의 생명체와 마찬가지로 지구가 살아 있는 존재이거나 유기물이라고 주장하는 자신들의 조사 내용을 발표했다. 이런 과학자 중 일부는 한 발 더 나아가 지구도 감정을 가진 것처럼 보인다고 말한다.

우리는 공기를 호흡하지만, 지구는 에너지를 호흡하는 것처럼 보인다. 러시아 과학자들은 강력한 관찰 장치, 망원경, 기타 과학 도구를 통해 지구가 매일 들이쉬고 내쉬는 에너지를 측정했다. 그들은 지역에 따라 약간 다르게 호흡한다는 사실을 발견했다. 지구는 인간처럼 밤에는 천천히 조용하게 호흡한다. 하지만, 날이 새면 첫 아침 호흡을 시작으로 더욱 깊이 호흡하기 시작한다. 지구도 마치 사람처럼 잠에서 깨어 나는 듯하다. 과학자들은 지구의 급작스럽고 빠른 호흡 속도로 지구가 깨어 나는 시간을 식별할 수 있다. 그들은 이런 방식으로 지구가 잠자는 시간 또한 구분할 수 있다.

흥미로운 사실은 지구가 얼마나 인간사(人間事)에 반응하는 지

이다. 과학자들은 전쟁이 일어날 때 지구가 마치 걱정하거나 화난 것처럼 아주 빠르게 호흡한다는 사실을 밝혀냈다. 그러나 전 세계 사람들이 명절을 축하하거나 긴장을 풀고 쉴 때면 지구 또한 편안해한다. 러시아 과학자들에 따르면, 과학자들이 이런 사실로부터 사람들이 알기를 원하는 가장 중요한 교훈은 지구가 우리의 존재를 느낀다는 사실이다. 지구는 우리의 행복과 평온함, 두려움까지도 느낀다. 이런 연구를 바탕으로 볼 때 지구는 우리가 싸우는 것을 원하지 않는 것 같다. 지구는 우리가 행복하고 평화롭기를 원한다. 러시아 과학자들의 주장을 믿든 믿지 않던 이런 가정은 꽤 일리가 있는 것 같다.

● **해설**

1 이 글의 주요 내용은 무엇인가?
　a. 러시아 과학계와 그들이 세운 일부 가설
　b. 지구가 행복을 느끼고 때로는 걱정하거나 화를 내는 이유
　c. 지구의 호흡량을 측정하는 데 필요한 과학 도구
　d. 지구가 호흡하고 다른 생명체처럼 감정이 있다는 가정
　e. 때때로 지구가 사람들에게 화를 내는 이유에 대한 상세한 설명

2 빈칸에 들어갈 가장 적절한 말은 무엇인가?
　a. 축을 중심으로 돈다
　b. 에너지의 영향을 받는다
　c. 인간사에 반응한다
　d. 사람들을 감싼다
　e. 그 모습을 바꾼다

3 "hypothesis"의 뜻에 가장 가까운 단어는 무엇인가?
　a. 증거
　b. 의구심
　c. 제안
　d. 확언
　e. 비망록

4 밑줄 친 "it"이 가리키는 대상이 다른 것을 고르시오.

5 이 글에서 유추할 수 있는 내용은 무엇인가?
　a. 지구의 감정은 사람들에게 큰 영향을 미친다.
　b. 지구 활동은 사람들의 행동에 따라 변할 수 있다.
　c. 지구의 모든 지역은 사람들과 상호작용한다.
　d. 인간은 지구에 사는 다른 유기체보다 지적이다.
　e. 지구는 국가에 대항해 전쟁을 일으키는 사람에게 격렬하게 반응한다.

● **구문해설**

3행_ They summarized their findings by saying the Earth is a living thing or organism just like humans, trees, plants, bacteria, and all other types of life that the Earth supports.
⇨ saying과 the Earth 사이에 접속사 that이 생략되었다. that은 목적격 관계대명사로 선행사는 all other types of life이다.

12행_ it begins to breathe heavier <u>starting with its first morning breath</u>

⇨ it은 the Earth를 나타내며, starting with its first morning breath는 분사구문으로 의미상의 주어는 it(the Earth)이다.

13행_ <u>It</u> seems that <u>the Earth wakes up just like people do.</u>
　　　가주어　　　　　　　　　진주어

⇨ like는 접속사로 '~와 똑같이, ~처럼'이라는 의미이다.

20행_ the most important lesson (that they want humans to learn from this) is that the Earth feels us

⇨ 첫 번째 that은 목적격 관계대명사로 형용사절을 이끌어 선행사이자 주어인 the most important lesson을 수식하고 있다. 이 문장의 본동사는 is이다. 두 번째 that은 접속사로 주격 보어 역할을 하는 명사절을 이끌고 있다.

UNIT 15-2　What Do Plants Like?

○ 정답

1. e　2. a　3. d　4. e　5. to see what makes them nervous, calm, and excited

○ 해석

많은 학생들이 과학 프로젝트를 수행하기 위해 식물을 대상으로 실험을 한다. 과학자들 또한 그렇게 한다. 거짓말 탐지기에 대해 들어본 적이 있는가? 거짓말 탐지기는 거짓말을 하는지 하지 않는지 알아내기 위해 경찰이 사람들에게 연결시키는 장치이다. 거짓말 탐지기는 사람의 몸에 있는 에너지를 느낄 수 있다. 사람의 에너지가 빠르게 움직이면 긴장하고 있다는 뜻으로 거짓말을 하고 있을 가능성이 있다. 에너지가 서서히 일정하게 움직이면은 마음이 편안하고 아마도 속이고 있지 않을 것이다.
과학자들은 이 똑같은 기계를 식물에 부착했다. 물론 식물이 거짓말을 하는지 하지 않는지 알아볼 목적이 아니었다. 과학자들은 기계를 식물에 달아서 식물을 긴장하게 만들고, 차분하게 만들고, 흥분하게 만드는 원인을 조사한다. 과학자들은 흥미로운 사실을 많이 발견했다. 우선, 회를 뜨기 위해 살아 있는 물고기를 자르거나 살아 있는 바다 가재를 끓이면 식물이 매우 화를 낸다는 사실을 발견했다. 식물은 살아 있는 바다 생물이 느끼는 두려움에 반응하는 듯하다.
이와 똑같이 흥미로운 사실로, 과학자들은 주인이 집에 돌아올 때 식물이 실제로 흥분한다는 사실을 밝혀냈다. 훨씬 흥미로운 점은, 주인이 귀가하기 위해 사무실을 떠나는 순간에 식물이 흥분한다는 사실이다. 식물이 주인과 긴밀하게 연결되어 있어서 귀가하려는 주인의 의도를 알아낼 수 있는 것 같다.

주인이 식물을 다듬으려고 가위를 꺼내면 식물은 화를 낸다. 과학자들은 식물을 속여서 그들을 자르는 시늉을 했다. 이런 경우에는 식물들이 긴장하지 않았다. 마치 식물이 주인의 마음을 읽을 수 있는 것처럼 보였다. 식물은 자신이 잘리지 않으리라는 것을 알았던 것이다. 따라서 식물을 돌볼 때는 식물이 예민하고, 똑똑하고, 아마도 상당한 초능력을 갖추고 있으리라는 점을 기억해라.

○ 해설

1 이 글의 주요 내용은 무엇인가?
　a. 식물의 감정을 탐지하는 거짓말 탐지기
　b. 식물의 지능을 강조하는 일부 연구
　c. 식물이 다른 생물과 상호작용한다는 점을 보여 주는 일부 연구 결과
　d. 주인의 심경 변화에 지대한 영향을 미치는 식물
　e. 식물의 의식을 보여 주는 일부 연구

2 "intriguing"의 뜻에 가장 가까운 단어는 무엇인가?
　a. 호기심이 이는
　b. 지루한
　c. 믿을 수 있는
　d. 독점적인
　e. 매우 싫은

3 다음 문장이 들어갈 가장 적절한 곳은 어디인가?

> 또한 식물들은 잘리는 것을 좋아하지 않는 것처럼 보인다.

4 이 글에서 유추할 수 있는 것은 무엇인가?
　a. 식물은 위협을 받을 때 반격할지 모른다.
　b. 식물은 혼자 있을 때 더욱 편안해할 것이다.
　c. 식물은 기분이 나쁠 때 시들지도 모른다.
　d. 식물은 신선한 공기와 햇빛이 드는 장소를 좋아한다.
　e. 식물은 언제 주인이 자신을 보살피지 않는지 알 것이다.

5 과학자들이 식물에 거짓말 탐지기를 부착한 이유는 무엇인가?

○ 구문해설

2행_ Have you ever heard of a lie detector machine?

⇨ 현재완료의 용법 중 경험에 해당한다.

☆ I <u>have never heard</u> of the story. (나는 그 이야기를 들어본 적이 없다.)

8행_ They put the machines onto plants to see <u>what makes them nervous</u>, <u>what makes them calm</u>, and <u>what makes them excited</u>.

⇨ to see의 목적어로 what이 이끄는 세 개의 명사절이 병렬구조를 이루고 있다.

14행_ <u>What is even more intriguing</u> is <u>the plants</u> got excited at the moment when the owner left his/her office to come home.

⇨ 관계사 what이 이끄는 절이 주어 역할을 하고 있으며, 단수 취급을 한다. is와 the plants 사이에는 접속사 that이 생략되었다. got excited는 수동의 의미를 나타낸다.

16행_ It seems that the plants get so connected with their owner that they could pick up their owner's intention to come home.

⇨ 「so ~ that …」은 결과·정도를 나타내어 '대단히 ~해서 …하다'라는 의미이다.

UNIT 16-1 The Changing Family

○ 정답

1. e   2. c   3. d   4. b   5. altering of the rules for adopting children

○ 해석

가족은 혈연이나 결혼으로 다른 사람들과 인연을 맺고 서로 밀접한 관계를 공유하는 사람들을 뜻한다. 가족은 대개 결혼한 부부와 그들의 자녀로 이루어져 있다.

역사를 통틀어 가족의 구성원이 달라지고 있으며, 가족의 정의도 전 세계적으로 변하고 있다. 서구 국가들은 가족 구성원을 재정의하는 데 주도적인 역할을 하고 있다. 미국과 같은 나라들이 세계 언론 매체를 지배하고 있어서 서구식 가족 구성의 추세가 전 세계적으로 퍼질 것으로 예상된다. 이 새로운 경향을 살펴보자. 무엇보다도, 서구인은 입양에 더욱 관심을 기울이고 있다는 것을 알고 있다. 많은 유명인사가 자녀를 입양하고 있는데, 현재 상황을 바꾸는 데 영향을 준다. 세계에서 가장 매력적이고 영향력이 있는 커플의 하나인 안젤리나 졸리와 브래드 피트는 아직 결혼하지는 않았지만 전 세계 고아원에서 아이를 입양했다.

가수인 마돈나를 비롯해서 많은 미혼의 여자 스타들도 아프리카 고아원에서 아이들을 입양하고 있다. 마돈나는 말라위처럼 가난한 나라에 가서 아이들을 입양하고 그곳의 고아원을 후원한다. 마돈나가 입양하기 전에는 아프리카인이 아니면 말라위에서 아이들을 입양할 수조차 없었다.

최근 10년 전만 해도 미국 법과 전 세계 고아원에서는 편부모, 결혼하지 않은 커플이나 친구들이 아이를 입양하는 것을 반기지 않았다. 하지만, 고아들의 수가 많아지면서 법을 바꾸었다. 이는 칭찬하고 장려해야 할 좋은 현상이다. 입양은 정말 숭고하고 멋진 일이 아닌가! 아이에게 사랑이 깃들고 안전한 가정을 제공하는 것이야말로 세상에 줄 수 있는 놀라운 선물이다.

○ 해설

1 이 글의 주요 내용은 무엇인가?
   a. 아이를 입양하기 위한 법적인 절차
   b. 가족의 중요성을 인식하기
   c. 전통적인 가족 구조를 고수하기
   d. 유명인들의 입양하는 방식을 설명하기
   e. 가족의 구성원에 대한 대중들의 인식 변화

2 "trend"의 뜻에 가장 가까운 단어는 무엇인가?
   a. 긴급사태
   b. 추론
   c. 추세
   d. 관용
   e. 에너지

3 입양에 대한 글쓴이의 태도는 어떠한가?
   a. 입양은 매우 엄격하게 규제해야 한다.
   b. 입양은 부부의 최우선 선택 사항이 되어야 한다.
   c. 자격이 갖춘 부부만이 아이를 입양해야 한다.
   d. 입양을 원하는 사람들에게 입양할 수 있도록 승인해 줘야 한다.
   e. 유명인사와 기타 유명한 사람들은 아이들을 입양해서는 안 된다.

4 이 글에서 유추할 수 있는 내용은 무엇인가?
   a. 입양 절차는 전보다 더 복잡해졌다.
   b. 유명인들의 입양은 다른 사람들이 따를 모범이 된다.
   c. 미래에 아프리카인들이 아이를 입양하는 것은 쉬워질 것이다.
   d. 전 세계적으로 고아들의 수가 꾸준히 증가하고 있다.
   e. 결혼하지 않은 커플들이 아이를 입양하는 것은 불가능하다.

5 "this"가 가리키는 것은 무엇인가?

○ 구문해설

1행_ A family means a group of people who are related to each other by blood or marriage and share a close relationship with one another.

⇨ who는 주격 관계대명사로 선행사는 a group of people이다. 동사 are와 share가 관계대명사절 내에서 본동사 역할을 하고 있다.

7행_ it is expected that western family trends will spread
　　　 가주어　　　　　　　　　　　　　 진주어
　　　 around the world

20행_ US law and orphanages around the world did not want to allow single parents, unmarried couples, or friends to adopt children,

⇨ 「allow+목적어+to부정사」의 문장 구조를 알아두자.

26행_ Providing a child with a loving, safe home is such a wonderful gift to the world.

⇒ 주어로 동명사구 Providing a child with a loving, safe home이 왔으며, 동명사가 주어 역할을 하는 경우에는 단수 취급을 한다.

UNIT 16-2 The Changing Face of Marriage

◉ 정답

1. b 2. e 3. a 4. d 5. d

◉ 해석

결혼은 서로 사랑하는 남녀가 맺는 사회적이거나 법적인 계약이다. 하지만, 낭만적인 사랑을 바탕으로 하는 결혼의 개념은 상대적으로 최근에 형성되었다. 다양한 문화와 관습에 따라, 결혼 연령과 결혼하는 이유는 매우 다양하다. 예를 들어, 고대 로마에서 많은 젊은 여성들은 10대 초반에 결혼했다. 중세 시대에 사랑은 결혼하는 데 중요시되지 않았다. 결혼은 단지 사업상의 계약일 뿐이었다.

지난 몇 백 년 동안 결혼의 정의와 평균 결혼 연령이 많이 바뀌었다. 오늘날 결혼은 우리 삶의 큰 부분을 차지하며 사업이 아닌 사랑을 상징하는 것으로 여겨진다. 일부 나라에서는 평균 결혼 연령이 높아지고 있다. 이는 사람들이 학업을 마치고 안정된 직업을 구한 후에 결혼하는 것을 선호하기 때문이라고 많은 사회학자들이 생각하고 있다. 직업적 포부가 결혼의 중요성보다 더 중요하다고 여기기 시작하는 것이다.

점점 더 많은 여성들이 남성과 동등한 교육 수준을 성취하고 동등한 입장으로 취업 시장에 진입했다. 많은 여성들이 결혼을 적당한 시기까지 미룰 수 있다고 생각한다. 이는 오늘날 결혼하기에 적절한 나이와 조건에 대해 토론할 때 고려해야 하는 요소이다.

일부 사회학자들은 미래에는 결혼과 가족 구성에 대한 더 많은 변화가 있으리라 예상한다. 평균 수명의 연장과 같은 사회적 추세로 인해, 일부 지식인들은 사람들이 여러 번 결혼하거나 일부 사회에서는 전적으로 결혼제도를 폐지할 수도 있을 것이라고 예측한다. 결혼하지 않더라도 자녀를 양육할 수 있는 제도인 '공동 양육'과 같은 단어가 새 어휘에 포함될 것이다. 일생동안 가족 구조에 찾아올 많은 변화에 대비해라.

◉ 해설

1 이 글의 주요 내용은 무엇인가?
  a. 오늘날 여성들의 결혼에 대한 생각
  b. 과거부터 미래까지의 결혼
  c. 여성들이 결혼하는 평균 나이
  d. 결혼할 때 고려하는 다양한 요인
  e. 핵가족과 핵가족의 점진적인 소멸

2 "outweighed"의 뜻에 가장 가까운 단어는 무엇인가?
  a. 비례하다
  b. 획득하다
  c. 오르다
  d. 취소하다
  e. 능가하다

3 이 글에서 유추할 수 있는 내용은 무엇인가?
  a. 여성들은 취업 시장에서 남성들과 동등한 권리를 달성했다.
  b. 오늘날 남성은 여성보다 더 직업 성취에 가치를 둔다.
  c. 중세 시대에는 사랑을 바탕으로 한 결혼이 중요했다.
  d. 과거에는 한 번 이상 결혼하는 것은 허용되지 않았다.
  e. 결혼은 앞으로 50년 이내에 사라질 것이다.

4 이 글의 목적은 무엇인가?
  a. 결혼의 좋은 예를 보여 주려고
  b. 평균 결혼 연령에 대해 토의하려고
  c. 사람들에게 노년기에 결혼하는 것을 장려하려고
  d. 결혼 풍습의 변화에 대해 설명하려고
  e. 과거와 미래의 결혼 풍습을 비교하려고

5 빈칸에 들어갈 가장 적절한 단어는 무엇인가?

> 사람들이 교육을 먼저 <u>마치고</u> 안정된 직업을 찾는 것을 선호하기 때문에 평균 결혼 연령은 높아지고 있다. 또한 평균 수명의 연장으로 미래에는 결혼에 대한 <u>정의</u>가 바뀔지 모른다.

  a. 기대하고, 조건
  b. 시작하고, 부부
  c. 바꾸고, 관심
  d. 마치고, 정의
  e. 열망하고, 나이

◉ 구문해설

14행_ Many sociologists <u>feel this</u> is due to <u>the fact that</u> people prefer to marry after they complete their education and have stable employment.

⇒ feel과 this 사이에 접속사 that이 생략되었다. that은 접속사로 the fact와 동격을 이루는 절을 이끌고 있다.

19행_ These are factors <u>which</u> may be considered <u>when</u> discussing appropriate age or conditions for marriage.

⇒ which는 주격 관계대명사로 선행사는 factors이다. when은 전치사로 '~할 때'라는 의미이다.

23행_ some think tanks <u>predict either</u> people will marry numerous times <u>or</u> some societies may do away with marriage entirely.

⇒ predict와 either 사이에 접속사가 생략되었다. either A or B는 'A 또는 B'라는 의미이다. A와 B의 위치에는 단어, 구, 절 등이 올 수 있다.

Unit Review **Answers**

UNIT 1

A-1 1. decimate 2. scarce 3. husbandry 4. descent 5. peninsula
A-2 1. a 2. c 3. d 4. d 5. b
A-3 1. antlers 2. terms 3. nomads 4. harsh 5. genocides
B-1 1. under threat 2. as a result 3. due to 4. a number of
B-2 1. figure out 2. are related to 3. wipe out 4. brought about
C harsh, herding, nomads, important, ancient, settled, tribes, arrival

UNIT 2

A-1 1. extract 2. vertical 3. chamber 4. ventilation 5. trade
A-2 1. d 2. a 3. b 4. c 5. b
A-3 1. blockage 2. gear 3. bottom 4. expeditions 5. spacecraft
B-1 1. in order to 2. in pursuit of 3. on top of that 4. up to
B-2 1. pass through 2. go on 3. bring up 4. clear out
C reach, deeper, dangerous, precautions, underground, constantly, proven, spelunkers

UNIT 3

A-1 1. heritage 2. barren 3. controversy 4. irrigate 5. mythology
A-2 1. d 2. b 3. d 4. c 5. b
A-3 1. dominated 2. cast 3. temple 4. staircase 5. attraction
B-1 1. as to 2. owing to 3. In addition 4. lack of
B-2 1. adds up to 2. dates back to 3. pay a visit 4. is made up of
C centerpiece, Mayan, sculptures, archeological, supposedly, homesick, fragrant, appear

UNIT 4

A-1 1. skeptical 2. fabric 3. mineral 4. grind 5. microorganism
A-2 1. b 2. d 3. c 4. a 5. d
A-3 1. comfort 2. silky 3. debate 4. chemicals 5. nightmare
B-1 1. First off 2. Needless to say 3. on the other hand 4. in order to
B-2 1. gone through 2. turn on 3. come up with 4. come around
C industry, advantages, environmental, require, innovations, minerals, act, widely

UNIT 5

A-1 1. advocate 2. manure 3. profitability 4. manufacture 5. confine
A-2 1. c 2. b 3. a 4. d 5. d
A-3 1. benefit 2. hormones 3. counterpart 4. minute 5. environmental
B-1 1. a large amount of 2. so that 3. in the form of 4. In response to
B-2 1. are attracted to 2. pay for 3. result in 4. do harm
C traditional, demanding, alternative, expensive, healthier, nutritious, innovation, yield

UNIT 6

A-1 1. appointment 2. earthly 3. memorize 4. utter 5. illusion
A-2 1. a 2. b 3. c 4. b 5. c
A-3 1. belongings 2. cognitive 3. imagination 4. influence 5. audience
B-1 1. for anything 2. in a row 3. each and every 4. a variety of
B-2 1. showed up 2. jot down 3. pick out 4. started off
C   Memorizer, remember, connections, tasks, hypnotizing, manipulate, single, skeptics

UNIT 7

A-1 1. master 2. assemble 3. inferior 4. cure 5. toddler
A-2 1. c 2. a 3. b 4. c 5. b
A-3 1. creativity 2. microscope 3. virologist 4. masterpieces 5. restrictions
B-1 1. Like it or not 2. at least 3. such as 4. a bunch of
B-2 1. is up to 2. are familiar with 3. made headlines 4. make out
C   sculptor, deadliest, understand, artwork, comeback, imaginations, limitation, pasting

UNIT 8

A-1 1. seizure 2. astonishing 3. infamy 4. request 5. sanctuary
A-2 1. a 2. c 3. a 4. b 5. d
A-3 1. exploit 2. Ironically 3. splendid 4. biodiversity 5. donor
B-1 1. in advance 2. rather than 3. thereafter 4. one day
B-2 1. get out of 2. caring for 3. worrying[worried] about 4. is linked to
C   seizures, epilepsy, python, everywhere, infamous, principal, rescued, shelter

UNIT 9

A-1 1. blossom 2. prediction 3. tranquilize 4. laboratory 5. synthesize
A-2 1. d 2. c 3. a 4. d 5. d
A-3 1. novelty 2. architect 3. organ 4. corporations 5. amphibians
B-1 1. in demand 2. in its infancy 3. or so 4. to name a few
B-2 1. pack up 2. make sure 3. is here to stay 4. be armed with
C   environment, health, observe, recommendations, future, wrong, widespread, foresee

UNIT 10

A-1 1. adorn 2. polish 3. quest 4. transformation 5. wilderness
A-2 1. a 2. a 3. d 4. b 5. d
A-3 1. perform 2. generous 3. congregation 4. recall 5. meditation
B-1 1. in advance 2. in return 3. at a time 4. Even though
B-2 1. refers to 2. prepare for 3. was rewarded with 4. been busy with
C   performed, adulthood, practices, modern, teenagers, formal, tuxedos, transformed

UNIT 11

A-1   1. continent   2. durable   3. reserve   4. migrate   5. caterpillar
A-2   1. a   2. c   3. c   4. a   5. d
A-3   1. exclusively   2. serpent   3. abundant   4. predators   5. sparked
B-1   1. at the most   2. each other   3. Even if   4. in fact
B-2   1. belongs to   2. feed on   3. swooped down   4. live off
C   continent, species, migrate, weight, exclusively, wings, predators, reserves

UNIT 12

A-1   1. alter   2. substantially   3. phenomenon   4. pioneer   5. conglomerate
A-2   1. c   2. d   3. a   4. b   5. a
A-3   1. contributor   2. dilemma   3. innovations   4. harness   5. solar
B-1   1. As a result of   2. a handful of   3. all the time   4. In addition
B-2   1. rely on   2. were tired of   3. go by the wayside   4. take place
C   long-lasting, pumped, phenomenon, human, environment, suppressing, alternative, pioneers

UNIT 13

A-1   1. gadget   2. emission   3. promote   4. distinctive   5. conflict
A-2   1. a   2. a   3. b   4. d   5. d
A-3   1. incline   2. metropolitan   3. innovative   4. navigation   5. infrastructure
B-1   1. along with   2. in that   3. as well   4. no longer
B-2   1. ended up   2. watch out   3. listened in   4. stands for
C   governmental, lifestyles, gadgets, delicate, navigate, researchers, promote, transportation

UNIT 14

A-1   1. chastise   2. satellite   3. fortification   4. superpower   5. liberation
A-2   1. d   2. c   3. b   4. a   5. d
A-3   1. compromise   2. nationwide   3. befriended   4. symbol   5. severely
B-1   1. a couple of   2. in control of   3. afterwards   4. In general
B-2   1. was driven out of   2. cross over   3. torn down   4. take place
C   symbol, divided, ambitious, constructed, reformed, capitalism, economic, cracked down

UNIT 15

A-1   1. deceitful   2. intention   3. inhale   4. telescope   5. hypothesis
A-2   1. a   2. b   3. b   4. c   5. d
A-3   1. scissors   2. nervous   3. energy   4. breathe   5. boiling
B-1   1. at the moment   2. According to   3. just like   4. as if
B-2   1. pulled out   2. make sense   3. takes care of   4. going on
C   determined, feelings, changes, hypothesis, experiments, excited, trim, carefully

UNIT 16

A-1   **1.** noble   **2.** dominate   **3.** glamorous   **4.** encourage   **5.** adoption

A-2   **1.** d   **2.** c   **3.** c   **4.** a   **5.** b

A-3   **1.** Statistics   **2.** orphanages   **3.** adopted   **4.** relatively   **5.** legal

B-1   **1.** According to   **2.** Previous to   **3.** more or less   **4.** due to

B-2   **1.** Look at   **2.** consists of   **3.** take the lead   **4.** do away with

C   changing, married, adopting, trend, rapidly, average, employment, distant

memo